Managing Child Welfare and Protection Services

Paul Harrison

RHP

Russell House Publishing

First published in 2009 by:
Russell House Publishing Ltd.
4 St. George's House
Uplyme Road
Lyme Regis
Dorset DT7 3LS
Tel: 01297-443948
Fax: 01297-442722
e-mail: help@russellhouse.co.uk
www.russellhouse.co.uk

British Library Cataloguing-in-publication Data:
A catalogue record for this book is available from the British Library.

ISBN: 978-1-905541-52-2

Typeset by TW Typesetting, Plymouth, Devon

Printed by Biddles, King's Lynn

Russell House Publishing

Russell House Publishing aims to publish innovative and valuable materials to help managers, practitioners, trainers, educators and students.

Our full catalogue covers: social policy, working with young people, helping children and families, care of older people, social care, combating social exclusion, revitalising communities and working with offenders.

Full details can be found at www.russellhouse.co.uk and we are pleased to send out information to you by post. Our contact details are on this page.

We are always keen to receive feedback on publications and new ideas for future projects.

Contents

Preface

If child welfare and protection services are to perform well, it is an essential prerequisite that they are managed well. Undoubtedly practice and management are inextricably linked; yet, like both ends of a telescope, they have an entirely different view of the world. This book views pertinent and emerging issues in child welfare and protection from a management perspective.

While many books have been written on the subject of child welfare and protection the vast majority of them focus exclusively on practice or policy issues. This book, however, concentrates on the management of practice and the task of putting policy into practice. As such it will be of particular interest to managers who wish to reflect upon strategic issues, supervisors who must implement strategic and policy directives and policy makers who need to understand the impact of their decisions on the service provider as well as the service user. It also provides a useful reference for those undertaking and delivering post-graduate education and training who wish to consider new and emerging themes in the area of child welfare and protection.

Using practical examples from both Britain and Ireland the book will challenge managers, potential managers, supervisors, policy makers, academics and students to view issues from unusual perspectives that are outside mainstream thinking. It reviews the context in which child welfare and protection services are delivered, provides an analysis of pertinent management issues and discusses current and emerging trends concerning the management of child welfare and protection services.

About the Author

Paul Harrison has over thirty years experience of working in children's social services. He holds qualifications in both social work and management and is also a member of the Health Management Institute of Ireland. He has held a number of practitioner and management positions within statutory social services in areas such as child protection and welfare, alternative care, family support, homelessness, mental health and addiction. He has also served on the board of management of a variety of voluntary organisations. He is currently working for the Health Service Executive as a National Specialist for Children's Services, with particular responsibility for child protection.

Paul has previously published with Russell House. *Managing Social Care: a guide for new managers* was published in 2006.

Acknowledgements

I am grateful to a number of people for helping me out at various stages of this undertaking. Thanks to Michèle Clear and Dr Helen Buckley for their advice at the ideas stage and for reading draft chapters later on. I am grateful to Eoin Rush who kept me on the straight and narrow in relation to children's services in the United Kingdom. Many thanks to Michael Bruton, Mary Hargaden, Eilidh Mac Nab, Mary Myler and Bernie Redmond for reading, and commenting upon, draft chapters – your expertise is much valued and appreciated. Thanks to Mary Ahern and Brian Harrison for proof-reading; and for checking anything I did that involved sums.

I am grateful to the library in Trinity College Dublin, which affords reading rights to graduates undertaking research; and to the Health Service Executive Regional Library and Information Service at Dr Steevens' Hospital, Dublin, which provides such an excellent service, on shelves and online.

Finally, thanks to all at Russell House for affording me the opportunity to publish this work; especially Geoffrey Mann who could not have been more helpful.

For my mother, Angela Harrison
who lived for her family

Introduction

The book aims to help senior managers, line managers, policy makers, academics and post graduate students to see child welfare and protection work in the context of the political climate, societal norms and professional values within which it is performed. It addresses the management aspects of determining need in an environment that has conflicting demands. It distinguishes between welfare and protection issues, the former often being misinterpreted as the latter by referees and service providers alike. It encourages managers to think outside the box to look for creative and innovative solutions. In this regard it promotes the concept of managing for results by using management information to design programmes that work best. The theme of partnership is explored in its broadest sense, from working with individuals to engaging communities in an effort to maximise effective outcomes. It makes a case for children to be protected from State care, which is a very blunt instrument by any standards; and protected while in substitute care because it can be a hazardous place for children, despite the best efforts of carers. Finally, the book depicts staff welfare as a management issue and presents ways to protect staff from the ill effects of working in such a pressurised and stressful environment.

Changes in the management of practice

The way in which child welfare and protection services are managed has altered greatly in recent years. The familiar ways of traditional supervision methods, expounded by Kadushin (1992) and Morrison (1999) among others have, if not given way to, at least been appended by, new management tasks. A whole new language has emerged to describe concepts such as performance indicators, monitoring, outcomes, quality assurance, value for money, information management and so on. Child care practice has shifted from a narrow focus of investigation of abuse to more holistic, evidence-based practices that are often required to be performed in collaboration with a range of professionals and agencies and to a pre-determined standard. There is, arguably, a risk that front line managers must inevitably reduce the original purpose of supervision (accountability, support and development) to a more restrictive version that is primarily concerned with performance management. As such, the original emphasis of supervision shifts from support for the individual worker to mechanisms that gauge the overall quality of organisational performance (Jones and Gallop, 2003; Statham, 2004).

Changes at the strategic level

The major reform processes that are currently under way in Britain and the Republic of Ireland, for example, require a change in work practice whereby managers are required to think and act more strategically. For example, in Britain the five outcomes for children as set out in *Every Child Matters* (2003) require an all-embracing view of service provision that is not confined to more traditional concepts of 'need' and 'risk':

1. be healthy
2. stay safe
3. enjoy and achieve
4. make a positive contribution
5. achieve economic well-being

Similarly, in the Republic of Ireland, the National Children's Strategy (2000) has overarching goals that emphasise what it refers to as a 'whole child' perspective:

1. children will have a voice
2. children's lives will be better understood
3. children will receive quality supports and services

Agenda for Children's Services (OMC, 2007), a policy framework for children's services, lists seven national outcomes, stating that children should be:

- healthy, both physically and mentally
- supported in active learning
- safe from accidental and intentional harm
- economically secure
- secure in the immediate and wider physical environment
- part of positive networks of family, friends, neighbours and community
- included

These contemporary policies surpass conventional concepts of safeguarding and protection and venture instead into new areas concerning quality of life. Neither do they stand alone as lofty aspirations; rather, they are grounded in reality by sets of objectives from which service performance and compliance can be measured. In overall terms good performance can be judged in terms of a service's ability to:

- Determine strategic priorities.
- Make difficult decisions about the service's capacity to deliver services within finite resources.
- Engage with service users in meaningful and effective ways.
- Support staff to develop and operate effectively.
- Engage with partners in ways that promote collaboration and add value to service provision.

Delivering services in the context of these reforms and performance expectations requires structural changes and well as changes in the roles and responsibilities of individuals. The heralding of changes will not, in itself, move hearts and minds: it requires the leadership and determination of a good manager to make it happen. Good intentions alone do not move mountains (Drucker, 1990).

The evolution of practice

Practice itself is evolving, and would have anyway regardless of legislation, national policy or structural changes. It is the nature of social care to adapt to changes in the social climate and the development of knowledge. The following are some key examples:

1. An illustration of change in the social climate is globalisation. The increase in global mobility has created a pluralist society. The diverse backgrounds of service users, and social care workers themselves, have come to characterise life on the ground in many metropolitan areas (Parton, 2004). Each brings with them diverse cultural, ethnic and linguistic backgrounds which naturally contribute to the evolution of practice.

2. The concept of what constitutes a family has changed. The nuclear family, as traditionally described, no longer represents the 'average family'. Now households and relationships are more complex and diverse. This diversity of family forms and relationships needs to be recognised in the development of family policy and the provision of services (*Commission on the Family* [1.8] 1998).

3. Another noticeable change in practice in recent years is the re-balancing of the relationship between workers and the families with whom they work. Interventions are shifting away from a fault-finding, inspectorial, model to a more strengths-based, partnership, approach. This is evidenced, for example, by the increased participation of families in child protection case conferences and family group conferencing that gives families a greater say in planning for a vulnerable child member, and the provision of more family support-style services.

4. Within the past decade emerging practice now demands that the voice of the child is heard and now represents government policy in many countries. Article 12 of the UN Convention on the Rights of the Child stipulates that children have a right to express their views freely in all matters affecting them, having due regard for their age and level of maturity. Several European countries now have ombudsmen or commissioners for children. Even in child protection scenarios children are now entitled to be involved in decision-making processes that affect their lives. This is facilitated by the increasing use of advocates for children who can dedicate themselves to ensuring that the child's voice is heard.

Not all practitioners embrace this partnership approach with children and families because it requires the relinquishing of some professional power. This is particularly so in the area of child protection where traditionally professionals saw themselves as protecting children from 'bad' parents. In addition, the whole system tends to be very adult-focused and it requires a significant shift in the mindset of workers to place children in a decision-making role.

There is, therefore, a job to be done by managers in leading staff to rise to the challenges that are inherent in these evolving issues of globalisation, family structure, the re-balancing of the relationship with families and the rights of children.

Governance is a management responsibility

When things go badly wrong it is often the management that is held to account rather than the worker. This was the case in the Climbié Inquiry (2003) which described 'a gross failure of the system' (1.18) and it identified senior managers, as well as practitioners, as being responsible. The report found that senior managers did not take sufficient responsibility and, as such, did not sufficiently appreciate the nature of the work that was being undertaken in the 'front office' (Parton, 2004). More recently, in December 2008, the head of children's services in Haringey was dismissed after a report, following the death of Baby P, found clear evidence of management shortcomings. The Ofsted report (2008) described 'insufficient strategic leadership and management oversight of safeguarding children and young people' as well as failure to comply with some of the requirements arising from the Climbié report. This demand for accountability in child care services has led to a new emphasis being placed on the role of management. It is therefore evident that management must take responsibility for the provision of strong leadership and organisational governance.

Governance concerns an organisation's accountability for continuous improvement and the maintenance of quality and standards in an environment that is committed to the achievement of excellence. In addition to the management of resources, managers are increasingly being asked to account for the quality of practice and there must be mechanisms in place to ensure that this quality is present (Cunningham, 2004). There is an onus on managers, not only to know what is really going on, but to be one step ahead of the posse, offsetting catastrophe by heading it off at the pass.

Taking stock

Most senior managers will have trained in another era before the pertinent and emerging issues above were even on the radar, so it is necessary for them to 'learn on the job' in order to keep up to date. Even less experienced front line managers will have trained at different times. At least some of the differences that this causes will manifest themselves on teams, with some members regressing to outdated theories and attitudes when they are under pressure.

On the positive side, managers bring with them the history of organisations and the evolution of practice and management. Yet, it is important, now and then, for managers to take stock of where things have come from, where they are now and where they are going. Therefore, the following chapters provide managers with a reflection of how services have developed; an analysis of the current situation and a projection of future trends in child welfare and protection services.

Chapter 1 explores the framework in which child welfare and protection services operate; having regard to the historical, political, economic and social issues that have influenced policy and practice in this area. The ethics base upon which child protection workers operate is discussed because the values held by workers directly influence the interventions that are used, and managers must be attuned to this fact.

Chapter 2 considers the concept of need and the definition and assessment of risk. The plethora of needs assessment frameworks and tools that have emerged in recent years are not, in themselves, a guarantee that risk will be actually, or accurately, assessed. This chapter will argue that it is vital for managers to promote, support and protect the professional judgement of individuals. Failure to do so runs the risk of producing a tick-box culture where professionals become mesmerised and incapable of doing the very thing that they are hired do to, namely the application of professional judgement to particular situations.

Chapter 3 supports the trend that is re-framing child protection work by moving from more punitive, inspectorial, interventions to more strengths-based approaches that engage families in a more equitable relationship. It also advocates that family support can be used as a protective measure even where children are known to be at risk. However, it requires brave management to shift the resource balance and operational functions from traditional child protection services to more supportive activities.

Chapter 4 illustrates that, despite a universal abhorrence and intolerance of child abuse, there is no universal definition of, or agreement upon, what it actually is. It also advocates for the invoking of the old fashioned principle of subsidiarity whereby state agencies ought not 'poke their noses' into family affairs without due cause. The destiny of families should be left in their own hands with unsolicited state involvement being limited to interventions of last resort. The necessity for managers to retain an overview of the whole process of child protection in their service will be emphasised. For systems to work effectively, managers must be confident that individual cases are being managed effectively. This requires the imposition of a system of quality assurance which cannot be delegated to front line staff and must be owned by management at a senior level.

Chapter 5 considers the need to protect children from, as well as in, State care. Even when it is provided at its optimum, care is not a very successful intervention and therefore should be avoided if at all possible. In most cases families are already known to social services and the admission is precipitated by a crisis that, in the eyes of the practitioner, necessitates admission. However, such scenarios raise questions about the level of attention paid to planned and organised preventative work and are suggestive of a lack of contingency planning. If it is considered necessary, care should be viewed as the most appropriate means of meeting a child's needs rather than an intervention of last resort; because a placement of last resort is not a good place to be.

Chapter 6 argues that results, the ultimate test of service effectiveness, are the responsibility of managers. Over and above national or organisational objectives, managers need to set specific objectives for their own areas of responsibility if they are to ensure effectiveness. It will also discuss the importance of strategic management, which is the art of selecting future courses of action that direct resources to the highest priorities or changing needs (Harrison, 2006). Too often reviews or enquires praise the work of individuals, or individual service units, while castigating senior management for failing to integrate the service as a whole. It is vital that managers keep sight of the bigger picture.

Chapter 7 explores the concept of partnerships. While Government policies, as well as practice trends, have recently cottoned onto the benefits of partnerships at an inter-agency level there is much more to be done to partnerships with individual children and families, and with the communities in which they live. Emerging thinking places children and their families at the centre with more opportunities for them to advocate, articulate and question. This chapter will argue that such a shift can move interventions beyond a one-dimensional child protection casework approach to more therapeutic, supportive interventions and, indeed, engagement with whole communities.

Chapter 8 asserts that, frequently, insufficient attention is paid by senior management to the toll which child welfare and protection work can have on practitioners and the long term effects such as stress, disillusionment and burnout, and it will expound ways to rectify this. It also addresses the anxiety experienced by staff in the face of demands such as performance management, target setting, monitoring and the standardisation of procedures; all of which can be interpreted by staff as a stifling of individual professional judgement.

As practice and management are inextricably linked, discussion in the following chapters inevitably weaves in and between matters of policy, procedure and practice. However, each chapter returns to central issues that are viewed from a management perspective. For, if services are to perform well, they must first be managed well. The essential aim of the book, therefore, is to provide managers, and those with an interest in management, with a discussion of topical issues that reflects such a management perspective.

CHAPTER 1

Managing to put child protection in perspective

Contextualising child abuse

There is no universal agreement as to what constitutes child abuse or, indeed, as to what constitutes a child. The term 'abuse' does not adequately describe a wide variety of behaviours that might range from an impulsive and immediately regretted smack to extreme forms of physical or sexual torture (Sanders *et al.*, 1997). Similarly, there is considerable variation between societies as to what distinguishes a child from an adult. These variations will manifest themselves in everyday matters such as when one is permitted to purchase alcohol, drive a car, leave school, vote and marry. A child, as a minor, may be over-ruled by parents until they reach the so-called age of majority, when they acquire all the rights and responsibilities of an adult. According to Hendrick (1997) 'childhood . . . as distinct from biological immaturity, is neither a natural nor universal feature of human groups, but appears as a separate structural and cultural component of many societies'.

These concepts of abuse and childhood, therefore, must be viewed against a backdrop of the socio-political landscape of individual societies. What is considered to be prudent chastisement of a child in one society may well rate as child abuse in another.

The social context of child abuse

The saying 'spare the rod and spoil the child' has its origins in the Bible (Proverbs 13–24). It implies that a child can only flourish when he or she is punished. In similar mode, John Wesley, the Methodist leader, is popularly attributed to have urged parents to break the will of the child and bring it under the subjection of the parent that it may be subject to the will of God. Influenced by a belief in Original Sin, this action was, presumably, designed to beat the Devil out of them. The extent to which such concepts are embraced or rejected will vary, not only from society to society but from era to era; for societal values are constantly evolving. It is evident, therefore, that child abuse is defined in contemporary terms that are influenced by prevailing political and popular ideologies in a particular society at a particular time (Buckley, 2003).

The rights and wrongs of such ideologies are ultimately set out in law. According to Ferguson (1996): 'Codification of laws and modern forms of social administration 'invented' social deviation in parent-child relationships to produce new kinds of knowledge of social problems like abuse'. In order to make sense of the protection of children at a particular point in time, one must consider the relationship between the social practices in a particular historical era and the contemporary concepts of risk, childhood, time and technological resources that were available to intercede with children in particular times (Ferguson, 2004).

Even within individual societies, there may be ambivalence and ambiguity in relation to what is considered to be abusive. Consider, for example, relatively recent debates concerning smacking in the home and corporal punishment in schools. The jury is still out in most European countries regarding the parental right to physically punish their children as a means of reasonable chastisement. Only one-third of European countries have actually introduced a legislative prohibition on physical punishment, including in the home. Article 17 of the European Social Charter requires governments, among other things, 'to protect children and young people against negligence, violence or exploitation' (European Union, 1996). In a landmark judgement in 2005, the European Committee on Human Rights found against five countries, including Ireland, for failing to provide legal protection to children from physical punishment of any kind from any source. European law is unambiguous; yet many member nations still fail in this obligation.

Outside of the home the position is now less ambiguous, particularly in relation to state organisations and those under state control. Corporal punishment is banned from Irish schools since 1982 and throughout Great Britain and Northern Ireland since 1986 (with the exception of private schools in England where it has been banned since 1989). However, there is quite a legacy to this current position. In times gone by there was plenty of evidence to demonstrate that parents, schools, institutions and the courts accepted a prevailing attitude that a good beating never hurt anyone (Maguire and Ó Cinnéide, 2005).

In Ireland, in more recent times, considerable controversy has arisen as a result of the number of complaints made by former residents of industrial schools and children's homes against the religious orders who ran them. This reached such proportions that it registered on the political radar, resulting in legislation in 2001 to establish the Commission of Inquiry into Child Abuse. In addition a Redress Board was set up under the *Residential Institutions Redress Act*, 2002 to make fair and reasonable awards to persons who, as children, were abused while resident in industrial schools, reformatories and other institutions subject to state regulation or inspection. The Commission was inundated with requests to be heard, the most common complaints being in relation to physical abuse and extreme corporal punishment (Commission to Inquire into Child Abuse, 2003).

Regarding the position in the United Kingdom, it has been said that 'Hitting people is wrong. But hitting little people, according to the current law, is not completely wrong' (Roberts and Roberts, 2000). The point has also been made that, in countries where they have come off the fence and banned smacking, the evidence is, not surprisingly, they are not overrun with 'sociopathic toddlers' (Roberts and Roberts, 2000).

Societal ambivalence regarding matters such as these is closely associated with the state of knowledge in that society at a given time. Many people will remember the emergence of child sexual abuse as a new phenomenon in the early 1980s. It was initially met with considerable professional uncertainty and dithering, before the development of knowledge and skills led to a reasonably uniform approach to the problem. Likewise, different societies can be simultaneously at different stages of comprehension and this militates against a universal understanding, or agreement upon, what constitutes abuse.

Qiao and Chan (2005) make the point that 'attitudes, not conditions, determine social problems'. By way of example, they indicate that in mainland China there is not yet a common language to describe child maltreatment: it tends to get lost in the vocabulary of child discipline or domestic violence. For many Chinese, the family is a private space where parents are traditionally endowed with significant parental authority and where public authorities are most reluctant to interfere in domestic affairs. According to Qiao and Chan, the public is more likely to acknowledge a social condition as a social problem if the following criteria are present:

1. It is perceived as having caused mental or physical damage to an individual or society as a whole.
2. It offends the values or standards of a dominant segment of society.
3. It has persisted over a period of time.
4. It has generated conflicting proposed solutions, with different sections of society making different evaluations.

This latter point reiterates the issue of societal ambivalence and professional uncertainty. In a country with a massive population and where rural poverty means that many children cannot go to school or avail themselves of affordable health care, the Government is bound to prioritise. As such, social conditions are unlikely to be considered to be social problems until the Government, not only has the awareness, but the resources to deal with them. Hence, it can be seen that social conditions and politics are inextricably linked and that social problems can only be accurately viewed in the socio-political milieu in which they occur.

The political context of child abuse

The political context is primarily expressed in terms of implicit or explicit policy and legislation, both of which provide an accurate barometer of the prevailing ideology of the day. As far back as the Elizabethan era the poor were viewed with suspicion more than pity, for they were perceived as posing a threat to the social order (Daniel and Ivatts, 1998). Attention was originally focused on protection from children, rather than protection of children, because they were seen as a menace to society rather than victims of it (Dingwall, Eekekaar and Murray, 1983). The Elizabethan Poor Law of 1601 is considered a watershed as it consolidated various scraps of legislation into one cohesive body. Essentially it provided for a compulsory poor rate to be levied in each parish and for setting the poor to work. Outdoor relief was provided in the form of money or goods and indoor relief could be provided by taking the poor into almshouses, putting the sick into hospitals, idle poor into workhouses and orphans into orphanages. The legislation provided an effective means of keeping an eye on the poor.

Victorian society, too, was pre-occupied with a fear that one day the masses would rise up to overthrow the existing order and confiscate private property (Woodroofe, 1962). It was a safer policy to keep the poor down. In the 1800s the Industrial Revolution brought a new order and a new discipline where 'the pitiful conditions of the little chimney sweeps, the vile conditions of the lunatics in the madhouses . . . were seldom seen, and seldom thought of by the wealthy classes of the towns' (Young and Ashton, 1956). The well-to-do were blinded by their new-found prosperity and comfort.

At that time there was no political will to assist even the most vulnerable or afflicted as they were seen as subjects of their own perversity, 'for were there not many in like pass who did not become parasites on the community, but whose guardians had foreseen and provided against such an emergency; or who through their own strength of character and resourcefulness had overcome the dangers of poverty and dependence?' (Young and Ashton, 1956). Over time this absolute position softened to a more moralistic stance where it was acceptable to provide financial or material assistance to the 'deserving poor' in order to help them overcome their moral failings (Parton, 1991).

The turn of the Twentieth Century saw the rise of liberalism and fresh thinking on the causation of poverty. Charles Booth, founder of the Salvation Army, published a major survey of poverty, *Life and Labour of the People of London* (1889) and Benjamin Seebohm Rowntree published his study of poverty in York, *Poverty, a Study of Town Life* (1901). Both works expounded the view that social disadvantage was a much more likely cause of poverty than idleness or moral weakness.

The *1908 Children Act* was a landmark in children's legislation. It provided punishment for anyone neglecting children, and made it illegal to send children out begging. Juvenile courts were established so that young people did not have to stand trial in adult courts. Borstals were also created whereby young offenders did not have to go to adult prisons. In Ireland this legislation served as the primary legislation dealing with child protection for over eighty years, right through to the enactment of the *Child Care Act 1991*.

Meanwhile, in Britain, the *Children Act 1947* was seen as moving provision away from the 'least eligibility' of the Poor Law to one which was welfare focused (Ball, 1998). Since then there has been an evolution of thinking and practice which moved the narrow focus of care for deprived children to broader commitment to the prevention of deprivation and delinquency, working with the whole family and caring for delinquents as well as children who are deprived (Packman, 1981).

Since the time of the post-War development of the Welfare State in Britain there have been a number of shifts in the delicate balance between the requirement to protect children on the one hand, and the concern to uphold the rights of parents on the other. The idea of the privacy of the family effectively defines the limits of social policy (Daniel and Ivatts, 1998). This is particularly so in Ireland where Article 41 of the Constitution provides married parents with 'inalienable' rights in relation to their children. In practice this means, for example, the parents of children in statutory care retain their guardianship rights and have a right to be consulted on all major issues concerning their children. It also militates against the adoption of children in long-term care.

In contemporary times the ultimate legal and policy development in relation to the protection is, without doubt, the *United Nations Convention on the Rights of the Child* (1990).

The UN Convention on the Rights of the Child

This Convention (CRC) is quite simply the most significant charter for the rights and protection of children in the history of the planet. Ratified by almost every country in the world, it clearly articulates that children should have first claim on society's resources. By locating this principle within the framework of children's rights, it is not dependant on a sentimental image of childhood or on an 'investment' motive (Daniel and Ivatts, 1998). It provides a much needed ethical rationale for socio-economic development that is not driven by economic growth and modernisation agendas (Affolter, 2005).

The CRC has led most countries to develop legislation, policies and programmes for the rights and protection of children. However, as a global convention the capacity and motivation of individual states to implement the convention varies. For example, in parts of Africa, despite efforts to improve legislation and policy in the area of child protection, the resources are just not there. In Kenya, for instance, in recent years, donor funding has been aimed at issues such as the prevention of human trafficking, the alleviation of poverty and HIV/AIDS. It is a feature in Africa that governments are 'bombarded with donor-driven agendas and demands' (Onyango and Lynch, 2006).

Over and above the demands of donors it is not unreasonable for governments, faced with massive social disadvantage, to set priorities that respond to some of the more essential and basic human needs. Citing Kenya as an example again, it is faced with an AIDS pandemic and a poor economy that have resulted in the majority of the population living below the poverty line. One million children do not attend school despite free primary education, two million children work and there are over one million orphans. In an environment such as this the noble intentions of the CRC are just not immediately attainable (Onyango and Lynch, 2006).

It is not surprising, therefore, that goals for the relief of gross social disadvantage tend to be fundamental and broad. In this regard there is a necessity for providers of child welfare and protection services in the more settled and affluent parts of the world to undertake a reality check and to realise that the basic act of survival must take precedence over the niceties of a refined child protection system. For example, in sub-Saharan Africa, some 12 million children are AIDS orphans, giving rise to the new phenomenon of children becoming heads of households. For them, Western-style child protection services are meaningless.

An expression of such broad goals is contained in the Millennium Development Goals (MDGs) that were developed as a result of the Millennium Summit in 2000, under the auspices of the United Nations:

1. the eradication of extreme hunger and poverty
2. universal primary education
3. gender equality and empowerment of women
4. reduction of child mortality
5. improved maternal health
6. combating HIV/AIDS, malaria and other diseases
7. environmental stability
8. global participation for development

Yet UNICEF points out that the children most at risk of losing out live in all countries. The exclusion of children from their rights to essential services is often a result of macro-factors such as armed conflict, mass poverty, disease (such as AIDS) and weak governance (UNICEF, 2008): but it can also be a direct consequence of Government policy.

Relative social disadvantage

A review of child poverty in rich countries found that the proportion of children living in poverty in the developed world had risen in seventeen out of the twenty-four OECD countries. Permitting this level of poverty that denies children the opportunities that most would consider normal is a breach of the CRC, to which most of the OECD countries subscribe. There is nothing inevitable or immutable about such child poverty levels; rather they are a reflection of how different national policies interact with social changes and market forces (UNICEF, 2005). It is a simple fact that there is a correlation between the rate of government spending on family and social benefits and the rate of child poverty. It has been contended that most OECD countries have the capacity to reduce child poverty below ten per cent without a significant increase in overall spending (UNICEF, 2005).

The relevance here to child welfare and protection is the extent to which Governments sign up to socially inclusive policies will affect children across a range of social areas that are fundamental to their well-being. Ideally, social inclusion needs to be incorporated into the plans and strategies of each government department. Progress in improving economic, social and environmental well-being is most likely to be achieved when national and local priorities are aligned (O'Riordáin, 2006). The raising of emotionally resilient, caring and optionally functioning children requires support networks that are capable of meeting their basic emotional needs for security, effectiveness and control, positive identity and belonging (Staub, 2003). Ultimately, at a national level, this requires a political solution.

Values and ethics: the cornerstone of practice

Societal norms

The quality and quantity of social services provided by a state reflect, by and large, the contemporary values and social norms of that society. Ultimately these values and norms find expression in national policy and legislation prior to being handed over to the delivery system for enactment. As these values and norms are in a constant state of evolution, Governments invariably play a perpetual game of catch up, responding to lobbying and public demand in response to emerging social issues and needs.

In dysfunctional societies, however, this balance may be impeded. International politics provides some of the most profound questions regarding what it means to be human. For example, there are instances of national leaders enjoying huge personal wealth while their people live in starvation and poverty, or where human extermination is used as an extreme means of social control or ethnic cleansing by one section of society over another (Moss, 2007).

Even in well developed, 'civilised', societies benevolent responses to social disadvantage can be interpreted as having an ulterior motive to secure the dominant position of the upper classes. In what he refers to as 'the positive functions of poverty' Gans (1972) makes the case that poverty and the poor may serve a number of functions for many non-poor groups. For example, he argues that poverty ensures that the 'dirty work' gets done by those who are prepared to undertake menial and undignified jobs to the advantage of the dominant class. These workers subsidise the consumption and investment activities of the affluent by virtue of the low wages they endure. This concept resonates with the argument, raised earlier in this chapter, that the prosperity of the better off requires that the poor do not acquire wealth as this would unbalance the prevailing social order. Gans goes so far as to suggest that poverty creates jobs for a number of 'respectable' professions and occupations in areas, for example, of penology, criminology, public health and (perish the thought) social work. In this way he asserts that the poor have provided jobs for what he terms 'poverty warriors'.

Cynical as this view may be considered, it does provide a useful reminder of the need for managers to frame the provision of services against a backdrop of prevailing and ever-evolving social norms. The increase in global mobility has created a pluralist society where values and beliefs have never been more diverse. The backgrounds of service users and social care workers alike have come to characterise life on the ground in many metropolitan areas (Parton, 2004). Each brings with them diverse cultural and ethnic backgrounds that add to the mix and, in certain instances, challenge what is considered by the majority as normative behaviour or practice.

In countries such as Britain and Ireland child protection services are predominantly a function of state agencies. While voluntary movements originally had a dominant role in this area, they are now more likely to be seen engaging in family support activities, leaving the hard edge interventions to the forces of the state. Child protection workers operate within a legal framework that provides a paternalistic approach to their involvement. Many interventions involve the exercise of social control, albeit in the guise of the provision of welfare services: because the bottom line in a direct intervention is that clients may be prevented from doing what they want (Calder, 1995).

Values play an essential part in shaping how interventions are delivered. One school of thought favours a laissez-faire approach which advocates the sanctity of the family whereby the state should not routinely interfere in its day to day life. As Smith put it, 'Like Sherlock Holmes' dog that didn't bark, it may be seen that the 'residialist' position in children's services can best be identified by the absence of intervention, rather than by its presence' (Smith, 2005). In a society where a developmental model dominates, the ideal level of prevention is primary, whereby improvements to social conditions creates an environment where individuals do not need to become clients. The institutional model, on the other hand, sees the state as having a legitimate role in intervening in social order so that individual or organisational malfunctions might be corrected (Hardikar *et al.*, 1991).

Child protection workers cannot be neutral on this issue; there is no fence on which to sit in this business. Key values such as respect and self-determination must be actualised in a practical context that inevitably favours one interpretation over another. Child protection work is legitimised by the state and the concept of welfare reflects the priorities and the values of the host community. The welfare ends that child protection workers pursue are directly influenced by the social and cultural circumstances in which they are practiced. Professionals must adopt a position in relation to the diverse interpretations of freedom and justice that liberal individualism allows only in the abstract (Clark, 2005). As observed by Professor Isaiah Berlin, in a lake stocked with minnows and minnow-eating pike, freedom for the pike means death to the minnow. In this context child protection workers are the wardens, licensed by the state, to keep the pike from the minnows.

Professional values and ethics

In a discussion on core values in a primary care setting McWhinney (1998) asserts that 'traditions are the bearers of values'. Where there is a living tradition there is a perennial debate regarding how the inherent goods of the tradition are to be realised. He argues that the healing relationship between clinician and patient can take place alongside others in which there are strong obligations and mutual commitments such as those between a parent and a child or a teacher and a pupil. A value is something we hold dear; something we see as important and worthy of safeguarding. In the context of social work 'values are one of those things that we will need to wrestle with for as long as we practice' (Thompson, 2005). In order to fully understand how we might interact with and treat people in the helping relationship it is worth briefly re-visiting one of the great architects of the casework relationship, Felix Paul Biestek.

The seven principles constructed by Biestek (1961) were:
1. individualisation
2. purposeful expression of feeling
3. controlled emotional involvement
4. acceptance
5. non-judgemental attitude
6. client self-determination, and
7. confidentiality

These principles provide a foundation of a value base for the helping profession that is as relevant now as it was the day it was written. Of course, not all of these principles are absolute and ethical dilemmas can lurk in their interpretation. For example, confidentiality is often qualified and, in the context of child protection, a parent's right to self-determination may well be thwarted by an intervention to protect a child that runs counter to that parent's wishes. In this regard, conflicts are never far away and tensions are the rule rather than the exception (Clark, 2000).

Even if one is working in an environment where an element of social control is inevitable, Clark has devised eight principles of good practice that are equally applicable in such situations:

1. respect
2. honesty and truth
3. knowledge and skill
4. care and diligence
5. effectiveness and helpfulness
6. legitimacy and authority
7. collaboration and accountability
8. reputation and creditability

(Clark, 2000)

Ethics are concerned with the way in which one should behave in a particular situation. Inevitably it requires a judgment call whereby one is attempting to achieve the most good and the least harm. Yet this is not straightforward; people will disagree as to what is good and what is harmful. As with the earlier discussion on smacking and corporal punishment, what is considered chastisement in one may be considered as abusive to another. The concept of ethical practice is not as well developed or understood in social care as it is in the nursing or medical professions, areas of which are commonly governed, for example, by hospital ethics committees and research ethics committees. Within the area of child welfare and protection there is ample opportunity for ethical dilemmas, disagreements and opposing views on how to proceed.

To take a case example: a sixteen year old girl confides with her key worker in a residential home that she is HIV positive, but she states categorically that she does not want her social worker or her parents to know. The key worker, provided with this unsolicited information has to weigh up the girl's right to confidentiality and self-determination with the right of others to know and to determine what is in the common good. While he ponders this dilemma the girl approaches him again with further information: she is pregnant. Now the stakes are higher because the rights of the unborn child must be considered. If this conundrum were put to two different child protection teams it is a safe bet that there would be disagreement within and between them. The point here is not to adjudicate on the case in question but to highlight that it is necessary to develop a standardised methodology for ethical decision-making.

According to Reamer (1998) ethical issues have always been a central feature for social

workers as they grapple with matters of right and wrong and matters of duty and obligation. He cites four major, sometimes overlapping, periods for social work:
1. the morality period
2. the values period
3. the ethical theory and decision-making period
4. the ethical standards and risk management period

In the 1940s and 1950s the moral concerns of social workers gave way to consideration of values and ethics. In the 1960s and 1970s social workers concerned themselves with issues of social reform, social justice and civil rights. These phases, by and large, correspond with the socio-political eras discussed earlier in this chapter. We are currently in the period of ethical standards and risk management that are now often governed by professional codes of ethics.

Codes of ethics

The most global expression of ethics in social work is the 2004 *Ethics in Social Work, Statement of Principles* developed jointly by the International Federation of Social Work (IFSW) and the International Association of Schools of Social Work (IASSW). It takes as its starting point its previously adopted definition of social work:

> *The social work profession promotes social change, problem solving in human relationships and the empowerment and liberation of people to enhance well-being. Utilising theories of human behaviour and social systems, social work intervenes at the points where people interact with their environments. Principles of human rights and social justice are fundamental to social work.*

(IFSW/IASSW, 2004)

The principles cited in this Statement cover human rights and human dignity, social justice and professional conduct. Many countries have developed their own Codes of Practice that are largely compatible with the IFSW Statement. In fact, the Irish Association of Social Workers simply adopted it in its entirety.

In the United States of America, the National Association of Social Workers produced a new Code of Ethics (1996) in response to a perceived need to be more responsive to ethical issues facing social work, not only in practice but also in areas of education, research and management. It provides guidance on ethical dilemmas that can occur in every day practice. According to Reamer (1998) there are three primary areas of ethical concern:
1. What might be considered to be a mistake, such as inadvertently identifying a client in public.
2. Ethical misconduct such as the sexual exploitation of clients or conflict of interest.
3. Difficult ethical issues that have reasonable arguments for and against.

This last point is more likely to present difficulties, such as ethical conundrums where the right course of action is on the one hand not easy to find, and on the other wide open to contradiction. As Mattison (2000) points out, ethical decisions not only involve distinguishing right and wrong but are also likely to involve choosing possible courses of action each of which offers potential benefits. Such realities are daily dilemmas for managers when, for example, prioritising service delivery options in the light of available resources. This is increasingly so when managers are being held responsible for the decisions that they make in this regard.

The British Association of Social Workers issued a Code of Ethics for Social Work (BASW, 2002) which sets out five fundamental values, namely, human dignity and worth, social justice, service to humanity, integrity and competence. In pursuit of these values it is generally accepted that social workers have a virtual obligation to advocate for clients by, for example, pointing out resource deficits where they are adversely affecting people in need. Managers, on the other hand, who are charged with spreading thin resources as equitably as possible, are more likely to describe the glass being half full. In this regard the two perspectives are not fully compatible with each other (Harrison, 2006).

Regardless of organisational constraints in the form of rules, regulations and culture, front line workers exercise a substantial degree of autonomy because the application of value-based judgements inevitably involves individual beliefs, perceptions and attitudes. To a large extent professional practitioners have a dual loyalty to their service organisation and their profession. Membership of a professional grouping brings with it an alternative power base that is independent of the authority of the executive arm of the organisation (Austin, 2002).

Child protection workers have another source of power: that is the power they can exercise over their clients. Particularly in child protection work there is an inequitable relationship between the caseworker and the client, especially when the relationship is involuntary. This provides the child protection worker with a double-edged sword (power over the client and autonomy from the employer) which, if wielded improperly, can cause serious damage. It is, therefore, a management function to provide the necessary checks and balances to ensure that this power is used responsibly. There is a perpetual tension for managers in walking the line between giving workers their head and permitting them to loose their head. This begs the question: do social care managers need their own ethical standards?

Managers and ethics

According to Dawson and Butler (2003) social care managers do need their own ethical framework because they are constantly faced with competing demands that need to be placed into some sort of order against a backdrop of restricted resources. Healy and Pine (2007) suggest that the publicity surrounding scandals in social services have contributed to an increased interest in managerial ethics. However, they also list several factors that are equally relevant:

- the emergence of new ethical challenges created by new technology, such as life support systems

- new health and social problems such as HIV/AIDS
- the increased scarcity of resources
- increased regulation of the profession of social work, with accompanying accountability mechanisms
- court decisions on professional liability

Managers are often faced with moral choices. They have multiple and often competing obligations to a whole range of stakeholders. They also have multiple sets of ethical obligations, especially those related to accountability for the public good (Healy and Pine, 2007). Managers act as role models. As such they can be an influence for good or for bad within an organisation. It is, therefore, imperative that they act with an integrity that will ensure sound ethical management.

In the USA the National Network for Social Work Managers (2005) has drawn up Leadership and Management Practice Standards based on the premise that social workers who manage use their professional training differently than those who work directly with clients. These Standards cover the following:

1. advocacy
2. communication and interpersonal relationships
3. ethics
4. evaluation
5. financial development
6. financial management
7. governance
8. human resource management and development
9. information technology
10. leadership
11. planning
12. programme development and organisational management
13. public policy

These thirteen standard areas neatly encapsulate the role and function of a social work manager. Specifically the ethical standards are as follows:

- Commitment to meeting the needs of clients within the purview of the services offered by the organisation.
- Commitment to the work and the organisation that transcends personal desires.
- Loyalty to the mission of the organisation.
- Commitment to the social work values of justice, equity and fairness.

(National Network for Social Work Managers, 2005)

In the current working environment there is ever-mounting pressure on managers to make efficiencies. This is often code for cost containment and the rationing of services. There is a perceptible shift from a focus on need to a focus on risk. This is manifested by the use of risk to target resources, the monitoring of cases and holding staff to account.

An inherent consequence of such a focus is the potential erosion of trust between the employer and the employee (McAuliffe, 2005). There are also the ethical choices managers must make in the allocation of precious resources. Therefore the concepts of risk and need are explored in some detail in the following chapter.

Main Messages

- There is no universal agreement as to what constitutes child abuse, or, indeed, as to what constitutes a child.
- Attitudes, not conditions, determine social problems.
- Progress on improving economic, social and environmental well-being is most likely to be achieved when national and local priorities are aligned.
- The quality and quantity of social services provided by a state reflects the contemporary values and social norms of that society.
- Managers need an ethical framework because they are often faced with moral choices based on competing demands against a backdrop of restricted resources.

CHAPTER 2

Managing gatekeeping and governance

In addition to the management of resources, managers are increasingly being asked to account for the quality of practice and there must be mechanisms in place to ensure that this quality is present (Cunningham, 2004). Governance is a management responsibility. It concerns an organisation's accountability for continuous improvement and the maintenance of quality and standards in an environment that is committed to the achievement of excellence. There is an onus on managers to really know what is happening at ground level if they are to retain oversight of the core business of the organisation. This starts with knowing what is coming in the 'front door' and how cases are being prioritised and processed.

The referral

Looking at the referral in terms of a business process, the initial contact expressing concern is an external event out of the control of the social worker who receives it. However this concern may not be taken at face value, but will be tested for its relevance to the purpose of the service provided. In an initial screening process the professional will interpret the perceived expression of need, or want, and make a judgement. The information contained in the referral will be considered in terms of its significance and relevance. It is worth bearing in mind that social workers tend to have a higher anxiety threshold than most people making the referral. A case that may have kept the referrer awake all night is unlikely to perturb an intake worker. This has been observed by others. For example, Dingwall et al. (1983) identified a tendency for social workers to minimise allegations of abuse. In any event, to make such a decision, even at such a fundamental level, the social worker must have a set of criteria.

These criteria are likely to be found in one of two forms. In the first instance they may be set out in official documentation, either prepared by the organisation as a whole or by a section of it, such as an intake social work team. In the second instance, the criteria may not have found their way onto a page; yet they are explicitly clear to the intake worker. That is because the criteria are learned as part of the socialisation process that occurs when workers first join the team: they internalise the team culture and norms.

Wittingly or unwittingly, the intake worker measures the concern against two domains, the relevance to the service and the capacity of the service to respond. In terms of relevance, there will be legal obligations or commissioning objectives in the non-statutory sector, to be fulfilled. For example, in England and Wales the *Children Act 1989* places a duty on every local authority to safeguard and protect children. Section 17 (1) stipulates duties regarding the safeguarding of children and the promotion of their welfare. Protection from harm is governed by Section 47(1) which obliges local authorities to undertake enquiries if a child is, or may be, suffering significant harm. In the Republic of Ireland the function is governed by Section 3 of the *Child Care Act 1991* which obliges the Health Service Executive to identify and promote the welfare of children who are not receiving adequate care and protection.

It is a relatively straight forward task to gauge the appropriateness of a referral against these legal obligations. Of course, legislative requirements only represent a minimum standard in terms of what might be strived for in terms of best practice. However, it is another matter to gauge the service's capacity to respond in a climate where there are limited resources. Inevitably systems of prioritisation and weighting come into play in the form of thresholds, or eligibility criteria.

Eligibility criteria

Most human services are performed against a backdrop of limited resources. It is logical, therefore, that what services there are should be directed at those in greatest need. It has been asserted (Calder, 2007) that identified need outstrips fiscal resources by a ratio of 3:1. Inevitably managers must make choices as to where the line is drawn which determines who does, and does not, receive a service. As discussed in Chapter 1, society must ultimately decide upon the level of support it is prepared to provide to various categories of children in need.

An audit undertaken in Northern Ireland found that all Health and Social Services Boards were influenced by Hardiker's framework model of graduated intervention from universal to highly targeted (Hardiker *et al.*, 1991). However, it found that one Board targeted services at families whose needs were assessed as being at the highest levels of the Hardiker model. Hence, an artificially high threshold for entitlement to services was created, thus excluding some children and families who, without earlier intervention, were destined to escalate to higher levels of risk and need (SSI, 2006). The Social Service Inspectorate report cautioned that 'child protection activity is complex and the framework model can only be effective within the context of good quality assessment and decision making at case level as well as appropriate organisational management of services which includes effective quality assurance' (SSI, 2006). Organisational management and quality assurance, therefore, are essential management tasks.

Such an emphasis on setting out explicit criteria allows service providers, in effect, to ration services, with the inevitable consequence of concentrating resources on a minority where the majority receive little or nothing (Calder, 2002). In this regard it is worth recalling Lord Laming's comments in his report following the death of Victoria Climbié:

The management of the social care of children and families represents one of the most difficult challenges for local government. The variety and range of referrals, together with the degree or risk and urgency, needs strong leadership, effective decision-making, reliable record keeping, and a regular review of performance. Sadly many of those from social services who gave evidence seemed to spend a lot of time and energy devising ways of limiting access to services, and adopting mechanisms designed to reduce service demand.

(Laming Enquiry, 2003, 1:52)

It has been argued (Munro, 2008) that since the Climbié report, efforts to improve practice have focused too much on administrative tasks, with social workers spending excessive amounts of time on form-filling and timelines and not enough on the engagement of people. According to Munro, the most startling aspect of the Baby P case in Haringey was the rarity of home visits and the lack of time spent in direct contact with the mother and child. One of the key features, highlighted in child abuse inquiries over the past thirty years, has been the necessity to make risk assessments and decisions with limited information.

In any event, organisations have a responsibility not to set out to exclude people as Laming asserted, and it falls to managers to devise creative ways to include as many people as possible. Social inclusion must be practiced as well as preached. The consequences of focusing sharply on the hard edge of presenting concerns are that the majority of cases referred are excluded; the tendency to only deal with acute cases is perpetuated, and opportunities to engage in earlier interventions are missed.

How social workers prioritise

Practice in England

Platt (2006) conducted a study on how social workers, in an English local authority setting, prioritise referrals of child concern. He examined how choices were made in individual cases concerning whether to undertake an initial assessment under Section 17, *Children Act 1989*, which provides for children in need; or to move directly into protection procedures under Section 47. He found that despite all the policy developments, the fundamental ways in which social workers evaluated referrals had not changed significantly. This is consistent with Spratt (2001) who showed that social workers were heavily influenced by concerns to address risk and appeared to adapt child protection techniques to working with child welfare situations. Clearly the volume and demand of cases puts pressure on managers to close cases as soon as possible where child protection concerns are low, even when welfare issues exist.

Platt took a sample of 23 families, concerns for whom came close to the child protection threshold. The study focused on three basic response types:

• Initial assessment under s.17 (child in need) procedures.

- Initial assessment as an exploratory visit to determine whether to use child in need or child protection procedures.
- Investigation under s.47 (child protection procedures).

The case analysis suggested that social workers evaluated referral information on five key dimensions:
1. the specificity of harm to a child or children (i.e. clarity and detail of the information)
2. the severity of such harm
3. the risk of future harm
4. parental accountability
5. the extent of corroboration of the referral information

The features that influenced social work decisions to proceed with an initial assessment outside the child protection procedures were concerns about the well-being of a child:
- For which the parent could be held accountable.
- That could be interpreted as constituting a risk to the child.
- That this evaluation was corroborated by other professionals or by previous social work involvement.

These factors appeared to explain how a referral crossed the threshold between no further action and an initial assessment. However, to cross the next threshold spanning initial assessment and investigation two further factors were required:
- The specificity of reported harm to a child (e.g. an injury or specific allegation of sexual abuse).
- The worker's interpretation of particular seriousness based on either current information or a pattern that had emerged over time.

Only a small number of cases in the study proceeded to investigation. Specific allegations of suspicious injuries or incidents tended to lead to an investigation even without other features such as corroboration. However, where this specificity was lacking but the situation was considered as particularly serious (e.g. neglect) an investigation would nevertheless be undertaken.

Corroboration and the analysis of risk did feature in decisions to conduct an initial assessment, but were not considered as so significant by social workers. The factors that tipped the balance in favour of investigation were specificity and severity.

Hence, the study concluded that five factors were used by social workers in evaluating referrals on the cusp of child protection procedures: specificity, severity, risk, parental accountability and corroboration. The focus on specific harm to a child, or the use of information from other professional colleagues provides a means of transforming uncertainty into a set of manageable decision-taking tasks. It was evident that it was easier for social workers to initiate an investigation under s.47 than it was to tackle less tangible cases that might fit a s.17 route. Platt highlights the well-recognised danger that, under these conditions, less specific referrals such as neglect or emotional abuse are likely to receive less attention.

Practice in Northern Ireland

Another study was conducted in Northern Ireland on decision-making by senior social workers at the point of first referral (Spratt, 2000). A sample of 200 files was taken where the senior social worker/team leader decided on how the presenting problem should be responded to and codified them accordingly. There was an even split (27 per cent) between what were coded as 'child protection investigation' and 'child-care problem' while the remaining cases (46 per cent) concerned relationship difficulties, housing, financial difficulties and so on. Spratt noted that while child protection cases only accounted for a quarter of all cases, they were 'resource hungry' as they involved multi-disciplinary protocols and procedures that create additional tasks for social workers.

It appeared in the study that referrals containing any level of risk were being subsumed into an investigation response; yet seventy per cent of the cases left the child protection system after investigation. This is consistent with other studies. For example, Gibbons *et al.* (1995) in a study of local authorities in England found that seventy per cent of child protection referrals were filtered out of the system and no further action was taken by social workers after the investigation. Spratt concluded that this over-identification with child protection had a number of unintended consequences. For one thing it is costly as it directs precious resources towards the time-consuming process of multi-disciplinary investigation thereby restricting the potential growth of family support services. Secondly, the over concentration on 'incidents' in child protection investigations, rather than a comprehensive assessment of the child's needs, results in support services not being offered in many instances.

The work undertaken by Dartington Social Research Unit (1995) reminds us that social workers do have options when presented with a referral. They have the choice to undertake a child protection enquiry; offer a family support service to improve family functioning; or they could provide a child welfare service. That report concluded that there was too much emphasis on child protection investigations rather than on more general enquiries.

Spratt contends that the use of the investigative response as a 'catch all' for the presenting problem may be explained as a rational approach to the management of personal risk. In other words, they seek to minimise the risk to themselves in the first instance, which has the knock-on effect of placing the child as a secondary consideration. Such a mindset, it might well be argued, may be a consequence of the fact that most of the big developments in child protection, on both sides of the Irish Sea, were as a result of inquiries into various disasters in child care management and practice rather than a proactive response to service development and professional growth.

A solution, according to Spratt, may be for front line practitioners to be given permission to make rational choices which would see the meeting of needs as being as important as the management of risk. This would require managers to promote the development of family support services and to manage risk by being prepared to defend such a policy shift.

Practice in the Republic of Ireland

In the Republic of Ireland approximately 20,000 reports of concern are made to social work departments each year (HSE, 2005, 2006). Following initial assessment fifty per cent tend to be categorised as child welfare concerns; the remaining fifty per cent being categorised as child protection cases, many of which cases are closed off after assessment.

However, the fifty per cent that are categorised as welfare cases are less likely to be closed after initial assessment. The majority were in fact offered, and availed of, a family support service. It is evident, therefore, that referrals of concern for children do not automatically have to go down the child protection route and can in fact be treated as welfare cases.

The argument is often made that resource restrictions make it impossible to lower eligibility criteria in order to facilitate less acute cases. However, this may be an over simplistic interpretation of the facts. For example, in Ireland during a boom period that lasted for a decade from the mid-1990s, the size of many child protection social work teams expanded enormously (some by approximately 200 per cent) with no corresponding relaxing of the eligibility criteria. The nature of the business did not change at all; the only thing to change was the volume of child protection cases which, paradoxically, went up. It is, therefore, evident that a management plan needs to accompany periods of growth that expresses the desired outcomes and the methodologies to be employed to achieve them. Too often the volume of child protection cases is used as a bargaining chip for more resources when in fact the reduction of such categories ought to be the prize. For this to be realised there needs to be a corporate strategy that encourages and values work that is conducted in the welfare stream that seeks to prevent cases from acquiring a 'protection' label.

Assessment

The purpose of an assessment is to inform future courses of action. It involves the gathering of information, an analysis of that information and the formation of an opinion based on the outcome of both of those processes. The nature of an assessment can differ depending on the practitioner and the service involved. The more agreement and consistency there is between practitioners regarding methods of assessment and the terminology used, the greater the level of understanding there will be between practitioners regarding their mutual understanding of the needs of children and for desired outcomes of children and their families (Buckley, Horwath and Whelan, 2006).

Britton *et al.* (2004) list a number of reasons for conducting an assessment:

- It is a direct link to, and basis for, service planning and decision-making.
- It helps the social worker explain their decision-making to others.
- The process can create rapport between the social worker and family through increasing better understanding of the family.
- It provides an opportunity to engage the family to set and achieve goals.

- It offers a practical way to utilise family strengths in a service plan to offset, control, or reduce risks.
- It encourages the social worker and family to explore family resources for placement, if necessary.

In the context of child protection assessment, it is necessary to factor in the severity, or the seriousness as described by Platt above, of the presenting problem. This will yield information on the extent of risk to which the child may be exposed. At all stages of a child protection intervention the safety of the child should remain a central and over-riding concern. Nowadays there are competing views as to whether need or risk is the primary consideration. In reality, like the dancer and the dance, they are inextricably linked.

Need versus risk

It has long been recognised that there are certain categories of children who are more likely to be vulnerable or at risk; such as those in large families with low incomes, those who are disabled, those in lone parent families and those living apart (Pringle, 1986). Often, in child protection, a combination of these factors is present. Pringle also reminds us of the basic needs of children:

- The need for love and security, such as the unconditional love of a parent.
- The need for new experiences, which is a prerequisite for mental growth.
- The need for praise and recognition.
- The need for responsibility, which is met by allowing children to gain personal independence.

Tunstill and Aldgate (2000) identified certain predisposing factors:
1. Intrinsic need – families which have a child with an intrinsic impairment resulting in manifest parental need for support.
2. Parental ill health – where the carer is not effective due to incapacity.
3. Families under stress – where the parenting is chronically unsatisfactory.
4. Offending behaviour – resulting in the involvement of the social services.
5. Social deprivation – where the need is based on the carer's own perception of their situation.

It is important to recognise that the needs generated by these five factors are not necessarily 'the fault' of the parents. Some of the needs are as a consequence of medico-social conditions that have nothing to do with abuse and neglect. Indeed, it should be recognised that social factors such as poverty, bullying and racism are also abusive to children but are seldom viewed in the context of child protection. In this regard Beckett (2003) makes an important distinction between three patterns:

- Premeditated abuse, to meet someone's need and desire where the abuse is usually deliberate and planned.
- Stress related abuse and neglect.

- Competence-related abuse and neglect where, for example, a parent is ignorant of the child's needs.

The needs resulting from these forms of abuse require sifting at the initial assessment stage as not all of these cases will need to be funnelled into the child protection system. The latter two categories have considerable potential to be dealt with on a welfare basis. As was evidenced in the above studies, some social workers tend to play safe by continuing to treat cases as child protection. Yet good child protection work requires the holding of one's nerve in certain situations. Managers who mandate such a response will find that workers can quite comfortably hold cases outside of the child protection system. In the above categories, if the causes of stress can be relieved and the ignorance be addressed by education and up-skilling, there is real potential for the well-being of the whole family, not just the child, to be improved by family support type interventions. These can often be low maintenance interventions that, once prescribed by a professional, can be left to non-professionals, such as family support workers, to implement.

Within the realm of child protection English and Pecora (1994) found certain factors that are common in such cases. These include:

- the child's age and developmental characteristics
- the character of the abusive incident
- the actual levels of harm
- the repetitive nature of the behaviour
- a history of violent behaviour in the care giver
- parental history of abuse as a child
- parent's recognition of the problem and ability to co-operate
- parent's response to the child's behaviour
- level of parental stress and social support

As discussed in the Introduction, government policy is encouraging professionals to take a more holistic view of the child. This is set out in the five outcomes for children in *Every Child Matters* (HM Government, 2003) in the United Kingdom:
1. be healthy
2. stay safe
3. enjoy and achieve
4. make a positive contribution
5. achieve economic well-being

Similarly, in the Republic of Ireland, the *National Children's Strategy* (Department of Health and Children, 2000) has overarching goals that emphasise what it refers to as a 'whole child' perspective:
1. Children will have a voice.
2. Children's lives will be better understood.
3. Children will receive quality supports and services.

The UK *Assessment of Children in Need and their Families* (2000) adopts a needs-led approach with the assessment process focusing on the child's developmental needs, parental capacity and family and environmental factors. Its fundamental principles, including child-centredness, an ecological approach and strengths-based partnership are all very laudable. However, it has completely sidestepped the concept of 'risk'. By so doing the government has, in effect, thrown the baby out with the bathwater (Calder, 2003).

Engaging in the business of child protection without the application of risk assessment is like trying to make omelettes without eggs. The whole point is to weigh up risks and opportunities and to make a plan based on the best interest of the child. Clearly the Framework reflects a noble attempt to re-balance child protection and family support. However, this relegation of risk creates a huge operational problem because, with the use of thresholds, the primary focus of intervention falls under the child protection agenda. This results in managers having to provide frontline staff with supplementary frameworks that are specific to particular presenting situations (Calder, 2007).

Investigating and intervening in child protection is by no means an exact science. It is less to do with verifiable facts as it is to do with descriptions of human behaviour that are open to interpretation (Munro, 2005). Risk assessment involves the systematic collection of information to assess if a risk exists and, if so, to identify the likelihood of it occurring in the future (Calder, 2002). Calder (2002) reminds us that there is no Holy Grail for undertaking a risk assessment: there is no definitive text or framework. Yet it would constitute reckless management not to install as robust as possible a system for the identification of risk. At the same time it needs to be recognised and acknowledged that no assessment tool will predict with certainty which situations are dangerous and which are not. Risk factors do assist to generally suggest what kind of situation may result in abuse, but none should be seen as an inevitable, or even probable, cause of abuse (Beckett, 2003).

It can well be argued that sometimes the very thing that children need is protection; thus supporting the case that the concepts of risk and need are inextricably linked. For insistence, Collins (2006) writes that:

. . . concepts of risk and need are both central to child welfare systems. Risk primarily but not exclusively is related to child protection and need also primarily but not exclusively is related to family support. Adequate conceptualisation and measure-ment of both concepts are needed.

Safeguarding

However, perhaps a compromise can be reached by positioning the concept of safeguarding between risk and need. In some regard it might be considered as a 'wishy-washy' title that is ill-defined and therefore open to interpretation. The second report of the Chief Inspector (UK) (2005) makes this point saying that the term had not been fully or adequately defined in law or government policy. However, it goes on to cite the definition used in the report of the Children's Rights Director (2004) where it is defined as 'keeping children safe from harm, such as illness, abuse or injury'. Walker and Thurston (2006) go further by describing safeguarding as a means of prevention of, and protection from, maltreatment; promoting well-being and ensuring that children and young people have options to achieve physical and mental health, physical, emotional, intellectual, social and behavioural development.

In the UK, the *Children Act 2004* provided for the establishment of Local Safeguarding Children's Boards, but it failed to establish a clear line of accountability between Children's Trusts and Safeguarding Children Boards, or how they might relate to each other (Walker and Thurston, 2006). This legislation also imposes a duty on local authorities and partner organisations to co-operate in order to improve the well-being of children. A successive finding of child abuse and death inquiries cites poor communication as a key indicator of what went wrong. Regrettably, despite the considerable organisational and structural reforms that have occurred in the recent years following high profile child deaths, communication within and between organisations remains a key area of difficulties. This has, for example, been raised in the context of cases currently under review in Doncaster.

In the Republic of Ireland the concept of safeguarding has not been developed in legislation or in policy. The *Children Act 1991* refers to welfare and protection. The national guidelines for the protection and welfare of children, *Children First* (1999), currently being updated, will continue to adhere to the concept of welfare and protection without reference to safeguarding. The first significant reference to safeguarding in the Republic has been from the Catholic Church which established a National Board for Safeguarding Children. It in turn has been influenced by developments in Northern Ireland, developed standards and guidance for the Catholic Church entitled *Safeguarding Children* (in press).

Whether the terminology relates to welfare and protection or safeguarding, the thinking and the strategic intent remains to protect children in the broader context of a child's life; and this is reflected in national policy documents such as *Every Child Matters* (2003) and *Agenda for Children's Services* (2007).

Assessment tools

Munro (2005) asserts that we need to ask of any tool 'Does it help the human operator to do the job better?' She also argues that the impact of tools on the nature of the tasks cannot be assumed to be benign; their introduction changes the way in which tasks are carried out. On the positive side assessment tools serve to standardise the way things are done.

In the Republic of Ireland there is not, as yet, a standardised assessment framework. *Children First*, the national guidelines for child welfare and protection (Department of Health and Children, 1999) requires that an assessment is carried out, but it did not provide an assessment tool with which to do it. This has lead to a disparity in relation to the way guidelines are interpreted and to inconsistencies in the ways services are provided around the country (MacNab, 2006).

Therefore, even with the reservations about the absence of risk in the UK Framework, it at least presents a standardised approach to assessment. However, Horwath (2002) asserts that the effective use of any national guidance is dependent on local approaches to implementation. Practitioners are expected to pay equal attention to the three sides of the assessment triangle (the child's developmental needs, parenting capacity and family and environmental factors) in order to safeguard and promote the welfare of the child. In this regard Horwath (2002) cautions that the assessment triangle is at risk of becoming a 'Bermuda triangle' as professionals and managers loose focus on promoting and safeguarding the welfare of the child. She says that assessments are being undertaken in a way that makes the triangle lop-sided. For example, in cases of neglect, when the primary focus of the assessment is on the child's developmental needs, the impact on the child is assessed but the causes in terms of parenting capacity and social context are marginalised. Similarly, when an emphasis on parenting capacity occurs, the professional perceives the neglect of the child in terms of an act of commission or omission on the part of the carers without considering the impact of the neglect on the child. She concludes that local strategies for change are as important as national guidance if managers and practitioners are to make the necessary attitudinal shift required of the Framework.

Management considerations

Managers are responsible for creating and maintaining the culture of the organisation, or their part of it. This requires the leadership of people and the management of systems. Managers have to make difficult choices informed by their knowledge of what is required by law. They need to be clear about the legal risks, both organisational and personal, of the options being considered. Managers need to have an acute awareness of the purpose of the service, as defined in legislation and regulation and to ensure that the service is operating within clearly defined standards (Madden, 2007).

According to Madden (2007), the initial challenge for human service managers is:

1. To develop relevant comprehensive state-of-the-art policies that reflect best practice, make use of outcome-based protocols and ensure that agency policies are consistent with legal mandates.
2. Dissemination of these policies to staff, reinforced by ongoing opportunities to retrain staff on staff policy.
3. Designing systems to monitor compliance with the policies.

Of course, staff need to be convinced of the relevance of the policies. A key strategy is to provide clear expectation regarding compliance and then to support staff in realising this objective.

Access to the service

With regard to accessing the service, managers should clarify the threshold for eligibility to services. This will be greatly helped by having a written statement of purpose which sets out the service's legal obligations, the nature of the service and how it may be accessed. Managers must ensure that eligibility criteria are legal and fair. Where legal obligations cannot be met due to capacity or other problems, it is essential that these are reported upon, stipulating the extent and severity of the problem and what efforts have been made to address them. If waiting lists are in force, a system needs to be put in place to ensure that no case on a waiting list is more urgent or serious than any open case.

Promotion of professional judgement

A standardised approach to assessment of need and risk analysis is required in order to achieve uniformity of practice. Associated with this is the management task of identifying and meeting training needs for new and existing staff. Any assessment model is only as good as the professional applying it. There is no substitute for professional judgement and managers must create an environment where this is encouraged. Child protection workers run the risk on a daily basis of being hanged if they do, in relation to intervening, and hanged if they don't where they do not. This, combined with a plethora of rules and regulations, creates a threatening environment for child protection workers where there is a real risk of them becoming professionally hamstrung, characterised by an abdication of personal responsibility. It is vital, therefore, for management to support individual workers by empowering them to use their professional training in the workplace without having to look over their shoulder.

Professional accountability

Conversely, we are in an era where professionals need to be able to demonstrate the reasoning behind their decision-making and that these are adequately recorded. The flip side of professional judgement is professional accountability. A mature workforce that has the confidence of management and has confidence in management will relish this prospect of justifying their decisions.

Monitoring and quality assurance

Managers must monitor, audit and quality assure the work going on at all levels within the service. As alluded to in the Introduction, the Climbié report castigated senior management for failing to take responsibility and for being out of touch with what was happening on the 'shop floor'. Front line and middle managers need to actually sample individual cases by examining files and interviewing staff as appropriate. One means of doing this is by randomly selecting cases and by plotting the 'client journey' through the system from referral through initial screening and assessment to full assessment, classification, allocation and case management.

Likewise the whole child protection system needs to be occasionally tested. Again the Climbié report referred to 'a gross failure of the system' (1.18). This entails having governance arrangements in place that address the discharge of mandated responsibilities and the systematic identification and reporting of any difficulties encountered. Delegated responsibilities become abdicated responsibilities when managers fail to have a strategic overview of the whole system.

Systems abuse

Systems themselves can become abusive in ways that can be harmful to children in certain circumstances. These include situations when professionals or agencies become more interested in their own survival and reputation than with the quality of the service and decisions are motivated by self-protection. It also occurs where there is professional reluctance to make tough decisions and where there are unrealistic interventions that are not sufficiently informed by evidence in relation to what actually works. Inadequate resources and resource rationing have also been cited as contributing to system abuse (Beckett, 2003), albeit that they may be issues outside the control of even senior management. Other factors such as staff shortages, high staff turnover, under-developed workforce planning, stress and overload also have a negative impact and this theme is explored in Chapter 8.

Performance management

The current preoccupation with performance management and national performance indicators create a danger of them becoming a means in themselves. Services are increasingly being asked to report on activity levels because the interest is, perhaps too often, on quantity and outputs. It can be very time-consuming and frustrating for managers and staff alike when there is downward pressure to provide activity data that subsequently gets lost in a black hole and never sees the light of day in the form of messages to inform practice. It is a far better use of management time to concentrate on positive outcomes for children where the measure of effectiveness is improved well-being in the child. It shifts the emphasis from 'What are we doing (process)?' to 'How are we doing (outcome)?'

Main Messages

- Managers need to know what is really going on 'on the shop floor'.
- Practitioners need to be given permission to make rational choices based on meeting need as well as managing risk.
- No assessment tool will predict with certainty which situations are dangerous and which are not.
- Effective use of national guidance is dependant on local approaches to implementation.
- Managers need to have an acute awareness of the purpose of the service as defined in legislation and regulation.

CHAPTER 3

Managing to promote welfare by supporting families

The refocusing debate

There is nothing new about refocusing children's services. For example, the transition from institutional care to community care is still well within the career-span and memory of many current managers. Provision for children and families is evolving continuously, with each new development retaining some of the positive aspects of the previous arrangements (Axford and Little, 2005). As alluded to in the Introduction to this book, issues such as globalisation, family structure, the children's rights agenda and the re-positioning of families from static recipients of services to dynamic customers with choices has altered the way in which services are managed and delivered.

It has been contended (Buckley, 2002; Buckley, Skehill and O'Sullivan, 1997) that the recent rush of progress, which is as commendable as it is overdue, derives more from political reaction to individual events than it does to the smooth convergence of a particular set of beliefs, values, policies and practices. Be that as it may, such progress is nevertheless welcome contributing, as it does, to achieving a better balance between the provision of welfare and protection services. It has been described (Little and Mount, 1999) as seeking a better balance between 'front-end' services dealing with prevention and early intervention and 'heavy-end' services aimed at remedying serious difficulties. However, the point is also made that this rebalancing does not necessarily require the dismantling of acute services *per se*. Nor does it mean that services should intervene earlier in a child's life; rather that they might intervene earlier in the chain of risk affecting the child's life (Axford and Little, 2005).

There is a commonality between the contemporary societal aspirations regarding children's services in England and Wales and the Republic of Ireland. In each jurisdiction the political intent is to aid all children, not just those on the margins. This is expressed in both governments' vision for children's services as expressed in the *National Children's Strategy* (DoH&C, 2000) and *Every Child Matters* (DfES, 2003). Yet, a variance does exist in the respective legislation. In England the *Children Act 1989* takes a needs-led approach by expecting services to respond with flexibility to the requirements of families. This is further reinforced by the *Children Act 2004*, which emphasises the provision of services for all children and the re-focusing of services towards improved outcomes in terms of their overall health and well-being. In Ireland however, the legislation could be said to have fallen behind the (more recently written) policy by confining services to promote the welfare of children 'who are not receiving adequate care and protection'.

Of course, like leading a horse to water, there is no automatic correlation between good intentions and successful outcomes. Parton (1997) argues that the central philosophy and principles of the 1989 Act have not been fully developed in day-to-day policy and practice in that family support aspirations are not being prioritised and child protection services are snowed under by demand. Indeed, it has been asserted (Tunstill, 1997) that this state of affairs is a consequence of the duty imposed upon social workers to pick up the pieces after every individual or institutional crack that appears in the universal welfare system. According to Ferguson (2004), within the current climate it is possible for the death of a single child to result in demands for widespread child welfare reform; as indeed was the case following the death of Victoria Climbié. He contends that risk consciousness has converted into risk anxiety for which social workers carry the burden. It is not surprising, therefore, that local authorities continue to give priority to families that are already known to them, with little evidence of a proactive plan to cast the net into the wider community.

In discussing the *Children (Northern Ireland) Order 1995* Pinkerton *et al.* (2000) say that, like the *Children Act 1989*, it seeks to achieve a balance in the relationship between the state, parents and children. However, they speak of confusion because family support is both a policy direction and a type of practice. In effect, the very concept of welfare services has been bolted on to the engine of a mainstream child protection system that remains the driving force, with family support on board as a backseat passenger.

There is also a difficulty in seeing family support as part of a set of terms such as prevention, family preservation, child welfare and social support. What it all means precisely may differ from country to country, with some seeing it as being in opposition to child protection (Pinkerton *et al.*, 2000). It is, therefore, worth devoting some attention to the core concepts that distinguish family support as a service in its own right.

Core concepts of family support

Despite the fact that family support shapes policy and practice in many countries and fits very well with the sprit of the *United Nations Convention on the Rights of the Child*, family support remains elusive and remarkably under-conceptualised (Dolan, Canavan and Pinkerton, 2006).

In Ireland the Department of Health and Children (DoH&C) commissioned the Child and Family Research and Policy Unit in the National University of Ireland, Galway (NUIG), to undertake research into good practice in the area of child and family services. This resulted in an excellent distilling of the literature producing five concepts and theories from which models and interventions have been derived (DoH&C, 2003). They bear replicating here:

Core concepts and theories

1. Intervention is appropriate to need:
   This supports the objective to get the balance right between protection and support. Most services have a mixture of services that include prevention, early intervention, intervention or treatment, and social prevention (to reduce the damage a problem causes). It cites the well recognised conceptual framework developed by Hardiker *et al.* (1991):
   - Base level: universal services available to all children and families
   - Level 1: services targeted at vulnerable groups and communities
   - Level 2: targeting early difficulties/early risks
   - Level 3: established difficulties/serious risks
   - Level 4: social breakdown/care

   Such a framework enables preventative and protection activities to be seen as complimentary to each other.
2. Child development and attachment:
   Understanding child development is an essential prerequisite to good child care practice. Here the seminal works of Maslow (1968) and Kelmer-Pringle (1974) regarding the basic needs of children remain highly relevant today; as does Bowlby's (1969) attachment theory which emphasises the necessity of secure early relationships.
3. Parental care-giving:
   The nature and quality of family experiences determines how children manage, not only when growing up but may also determine the nature and quality of their relationships and their overall well-being in adulthood (Gilligan, 1995). Therefore, to adequately understand the needs of a child they have to been seen in the context of their family.
4. Resilience:
   Resilience concerns a person's ability to recover from adverse situations. Children who are secure in supportive relationships are more likely to recover from life's setbacks. According to Gilligan (2001) some children adapt successfully to risky circumstances and, in fact, do better than might be reasonably expected. This may be due to the complex interaction of qualities of the risk and adversity involved, the experience of the child and the relationships and environment in which the child is growing up.
5. Ecological approach:
   An ecological approach affords an insight into the adverse effects which family circumstances can have on child development. It advocates that the family itself be viewed in the context of the environment of which it is part. The relationship between poverty and abuse and neglect is discussed later in this chapter.

An essential concept of family support is that it is strengths-based. It moves away from traditional perspectives of deficits, pathology and risk and is more concerned with finding, and working with, strengths within families (Gilligan, 2000). It is also likely to be multi-dimensional: in other words conventional casework is replaced, or at least added to, by a range of inputs working in tandem with each other. Alliances are important where different services, perhaps different agencies, join forces in a co-operative and co-ordinated manner, with the clear purpose of tackling a pre-determined need. Hence, a service compound is created with the unified purpose of tackling problems on a number of fronts simultaneously.

The objective, therefore, of family support is to empower families rather than to police them; re-enforcing their existing protective factors and compensating for those that are absent, either temporarily or permanently (Buckley, 2002).

Principles of good practice

In general, prevention and early intervention will be more effective when they are a response to clear evidence of need and are designed to address the causes of the problems being experienced by children in need (Little, 1999). In keeping with contemporary national policy, services should take a 'whole child' approach, not only seeing the child in the round but also in the context of their family and their wider social network. The opportunity should be given to families to define their own problems and needs (Gilligan, 2000). Focus should be placed on strengths within the family, not weaknesses.

Services should be alluring, relevant and accessible to potential users. For example, it has been suggested (McKeown, 2001) that the reason for the generally low uptake of services for fathers is that what is on offer is not appropriate to their needs or, at least, not attractive to them. Services should also be provided in places where children and families go naturally in the normal course of their lives.

Effective inter-disciplinary and inter-agency working, which is a hallmark of good family support, does not have to emanate from the same physical space. Co-habitation is not a prerequisite for effective partnership. However, partnership does require that services are integrated in such a way that they provide maximum effect. Yoshikawa (1994) remarks that it is not the number of services on offer that has a beneficial impact on families; it is the way in which the components are integrated and sequenced.

Hence, some of the broad principles underpinning family support can be summarised as:
- Interventions should be responsive to clear evidence of need.
- Families should be afforded the opportunity to describe their own problems and needs.
- Services should be strengths-based.
- Services should be relevant, attractive and accessible.
- Combinations of services should be provided in an integrated and sequenced manner.

Management principles

The researchers at NUIG, referred to above, also drew from existing research, evaluation and theoretical literature to develop a specific set of management principles (DoH&C, 2003):

1. A range of services is available, targeted at different levels of need, within a framework of prevention:
   This principle advocates a strategic approach whereby different levels of support are made available in accordance with identified needs, as in the Hardiker framework.
2. Services have clear objectives and a management and organisational culture that facilitates their achievement:
   A quality service requires that the service has clearly stated aims and objectives as well as the capacity to deliver upon them. A strong philosophy regarding how services should be delivered should be embedded in the management and organisational culture.
3. The service has a culture of learning and development:
   As there is no 'one size fits all', services need to be flexible, innovative and constantly evolving. For this to happen effectively, organisations need strong links to the latest research and a plan for ongoing staff development.
4. The service measures outcomes:
   In general, social care is notorious for describing what it does rather than how it does. It is, therefore, important for services to devise ways of measuring outcomes in order to measure the success of a particular intervention.
5. The service has adequate resources to meet its objectives and offers value for money:
   The researchers cite Darro and Donnelly (2002) who found that, in the USA, in a rush to develop more services, too much emphasis was placed on the breath of services at the expense of the depth of services. An essential requirement in family support is that services are provided in sufficient measure and for a sufficient duration. A non-professional family support worker who assists a family in key areas over a long period may well prove more effective than a sudden burst of social work activity after a case is escalated to a child protection level. As Spratt (2001) has commented, the response system in child care is 'resource hungry . . . Like the fire brigade it attends more false alarms than real disasters, but is nevertheless kept in expensive readiness.'
6. The service has a commitment to effective partnership practice:
   Partnership in this context has two dimensions: the relationship between the service and the families, and the relationship between the agencies and disciplines engaged in meeting the needs of families. In each case there needs to be open communication systems and workers from a range of agencies need to work together in a co-ordinated way in order to meet the needs of families.
7. Services provide good staff development and support:
   Working with troubled families is hard work. Staff need to feel supported as well as being adequately trained. Management also has an obligation to protect the health, safety and professional development of its staff (see Chapter 8).

In overall terms, be it for practice or the management of practice, the over-riding principles can be distilled into what Pinkerton *et al.* (2000) describe as the twin principles of the paramount position of the welfare of the child and the promotion of parental responsibility.

Descriptions and levels of family support

Concepts such as risk, need and prevention appear straightforward at first glance but in the context of policy research they require careful definition (Smith, 1999). At least until recently, policies have tended to be based on narrow definitions and specific incidents of child abuse, with the inevitable enquiries following any perceived failures to protect individual children from significant harm. In these circumstances there has been little opportunity to successfully refocus services based on a better balance between prevention and family support on the one hand and child protection interventions on the other (Jack, 2006). Prevention strategies are significantly influenced by the definitions of the problem they seek to prevent. The literature tends to prioritise a model of prevention which is based on a narrow definition of abuse and derived from specific case data (Wattam, 1999). There is, therefore, a need to overcome such a deep-seated, individually orientated, child protection-focused mindset if services are to be successfully re-balanced in favour of supporting families in the context of their own social networks and communities (Jack, 2006).

In considering preventative and early interventions, the literature tends to emulate the medical model that refers to primary, secondary and tertiary care. For example, Little and Mount (1999) draw examples from early medicine, such as the prevention of cholera, to support the fundamental logic of prevention: 'Far better to take decisive preventative action than to wait for a disease to take hold'. Yet, it has been asked (Smith, 1999): do such public health analogies fit well with the tradition of community-wide policies directed at social well-being and universally available to all? For, in this context, services are available as of right, regardless of their preventative value or their predicted outcome.

The Hardiker framework (1991), as referred to above, has four levels to describe a range of preventative interventions. The primary level refers to universal services; secondary refers to some changed thinking regarding preventative activity:

- Prevention to intervene with a whole population to prevent potential problems from emerging.
- Early intervention with people who show the first signs of an identified problem and who are known to be at high risk of succumbing to that problem.
- Interventions to focus on the particular circumstances of people who have developed most of the symptoms of the identified problem.
- Social prevention to minimise the damage that those who have developed an identified condition can do to themselves and others.

Interventions aimed at whole populations are more likely to be conducted as national or regional campaigns initiated at a corporate level, rather than at local departmental level. Examples of such primary prevention programmes are the public awareness programme recently run by the Health Service Executive in Ireland entitled *Parents who Listen Protect* and the *Cruelty to Children Must Stop: Full Stop* campaign run by the National Society for the Prevention of Cruelty to Children in the UK.

In Ireland, family support is usually defined in terms of direct work carried out with vulnerable families in their own home or community (Buckley, 2002). Its objective is to strengthen their well-being and reduce the risk of children being harmed or separated from their families. This is supported by *Children First: the National Guidelines for the Protection and Welfare of Children* (DoH&C, 1999) which, in support of family support, states: 'Early intervention can help to prevent any worsening of current difficulties being experienced by a family and will assist the development and growth of protective factors'.

This level of intervention equates to what Gilligan (2000) describes as 'compensatory family support'. Its purpose is to compensate families for the ill-effects of disadvantage or adversity. Such services might, for example, take the form of specialist day care for pre-school children or special youth projects aimed at young children who are exhibiting vulnerable traits. On either side of such an intervention, Gilligan positions 'developmental family support' which aims to strengthen the coping capacity of families in the context of their own community, such as a parenting programme; and 'protective family support' which responds to identified risks by, for example, the provision of a homemaker or a child behaviour management programme.

Dolan, Canavan and Pinkerton (2006) describe family support services as having seven components:

1. Integrated programmes combining statutory, voluntary, community and private sectors.
2. Positive reinforcement for informal social networks.
3. Targeting of the hard to reach, vulnerable or at risk.
4. Wide range of activities and types of service.
5. Style of work based on operational and practice principles.
6. Early intervention across a range of levels and needs.
7. Promotion and protection of health, well-being and rights of all children and young people and their families and communities.

These components illustrate that a distinguishing feature of family support is that it can offer a wide-ranging menu of intervention opportunities that can be delivered at a variety of levels, from broad preventative measures to services that are more targeted at families which have been identified as vulnerable. In this regard it should be seen as multi-dimensional. It is not one thing alone; it can be a range of interventions operating at different levels through formal or informal systems (Cameron, Vanderwoerd and Peirson, 1997). In essence, complex needs may require several services simultaneously from a variety of agencies. It is not helpful, therefore, if services such as health and social services place themselves in opposition to one another when both might be required to have the desired effect in the life of a child (Little, 1999).

In the UK and Ireland, government policy intent is that there should be a more proactive attitude to family support by what Jack (2006) describes as 'mainstreaming preventative approaches'. This intent finds expression in both *Every Child Matters* (DfES, 2003) and *Children First* (DoH&C, 1999). Yet, good intentions alone do not move mountains: the task of shifting policy into practice requires the spadework of a competent manager.

Managing to put policies and principles into practice

Child protection and public expectation

By the 1990s, in the English-speaking world at least, there was a palpable backlash against the perceived intrusiveness of social workers. This resulted in child protection work coming under close public scrutiny. At the same time, however, Corby (2006) argues that, in the context of England and Wales, the messages coming from central government over the same period were by no means consistent. He says that, having raised concerns over certain types of abuse, and having encouraged the re-focusing of services to more family support work, there was at the same time a widening of the range of abuse types requiring a child abuse response as set out in *Working Together to Safeguard Children* (DoH, 1999).

Social work has been caught between a rock and a hard place: on the one hand it is encouraged to move into a more proactive, strengths-based mode; on the other a political, public and media expectation remains that it should have a one-hundred per cent safety record when it comes to the protection of children. Social work serves as the sponge that mops up society's anxiety and consequently, according to Munro (2005) it bears its guilt for disaster and becomes the target for its frustration. In the New Zealand context, Connolly and Doolan (2007) assert that: 'increasingly high community expectations that social workers must protect all children and never miss a single case of abuse have driven practice towards increasingly forensic investigations of any allegation of abuse or concern'. Therefore, a hiatus exists between the aspirations of expressed public policy and the reality of public expectation. Consequently there is huge potential for what Calder (2007) refers to as 'track jumping' between strength and risk approaches to case management. Confronted by a critical safety issue or the non-compliance of participants a dramatic switch of approach is likely to be made. When the going gets tough there is, in effect, a reversion to type where progress gives way to old familiar ways.

The exclusion of social inclusion policy

Another disconnection between policy and practice is the lack of fit between national social inclusion strategy and the reality on the ground. Research has clearly established that poverty is the most significant factor that links childhood development with social and economic outcomes in adult life (Gregg *et al.*, 1999). In the United Kingdom, *Every Child Matters* (DfES, 2003) represents a well intended approach to reforming policy and practice, acknowledging as it does, that child protection *per se* cannot be separated from overall policies designed to improve children's lives as a whole. Yet the five key outcomes for children: being healthy, staying safe, enjoying and achieving, making a positive contribution and economic well-being, would require long term changes in organisational and professional cultures (Gill and Jack, 2007). In reality, the Government's emphasis on social inclusion strategies is not yet reflected in mainstream children's services (Jack, 2006).

Although not all poor people have social workers, nearly all the people seen by social workers are poor (Williams, 1997). This is no coincidence. As Parton (1991) described it some years ago: 'Social work essentially occupies the space between the respectable and the deviant . . . classes . . . It fulfils an essential mediating role between those who are actually or potentially excluded and the mainstream of society'. Clearly the thinking has moved on since this observation was made; yet the challenge remains to have it fully reflected in practice.

The location of the debate around prevention and its association with the individual rather than structural definitions has not helped to develop either a good understanding of childhood disadvantage or a policy to deal with it. Local authorities continue to prioritise neglect, those at risk of significant harm and those in state care (Smith, 1999). This is the case even in authorities where there is a clear policy commitment to developing community-based service focused on children's well-being. Davis (1997) found that in one London Borough a community participation strategy ended when a change of management reverted to a more top down approach to case management. As was seen with attempts to introduce a strengths-based approach, when the going gets tough there is always the temptation to revert to the familiar ways of risk management.

So what can managers do to effect a lasting change that, although generally seen as desirable, has not yet been successfully maintained? The answer lays in not only tackling organisational change, but in tackling attitudinal and cultural change as well.

Moving hearts and minds

When governments want to effect change they will invariably opt for organisational transformation. Yet this in itself does nothing to alter to mindset of those undertaking the core business of the organisation: it is still the same people pushing the same pens at the end of the day. Within the past decade change has almost become a constant in the daily lives of social care workers in the public service. Those in political power often go for the quick fix, leaving managers disempowered and staff disillusioned. In an environment where there is constant change managers can actually be impeded from managing, as it becomes very difficult for them to focus on how they should do things and how they can bring people with them. In reality a slow haul, involving consultation and consensus, is likely to be more effective than a speedy short-term solution (Devine, 2007).

Managers are in a position to fulfil the role of change agent within organisations. There must be clear accountability for managing the change process and for the decisions taken as a consequence (Learner and Rosen, 2004). Although managers at all levels are to some extent change agents in their organisation, the actual change process needs to be made the specific responsibility of a particular person, or group of persons (Kanter, Stein and Jick, 1992).

In effect, staff need to be mandated by management to be allowed to behave in a different way than they did before. In an exercise undertaken by Spratt (2001), social workers were asked to comment on the hypothesis that taking a child welfare approach, over a child protection approach, in the initial coding of referrals, would change social work practice. One third of respondents felt that it would not. According to Spratt, this response highlights the dilemma faced by social workers who, even if they commit to a welfare approach, are still mandated to address the concerns that prompted the referral in the first place. There is a fear factor that causes referrals with child welfare characteristics to be dealt with strictly in a child protection mode. Professional judgement and choice is restricted by the organisational context in which decisions are made.

A recent study of service users' perceptions in the area of child protection made the following observation:

> While it is difficult to see how a method of investigation can be found that reconciles the need to protect children in dangerous circumstances and at the same time protect their caregivers' sense of integrity, it is clear that not all children who come to the attention of the services are at serious risk, and we suggest that alternative response models currently being developed and tried in other jurisdictions could be given some consideration.
>
> (Buckley et al., 2008)

Therefore, a leap of faith is required by managers in order to enable front line workers to perform in a different way. The fear of being held publicly accountable for failings or short comings needs to be borne by managers if social workers 'on the beat' are to be empowered to take risks in order to wriggle out of the straight jacket of traditional child protection interventions. An essential prerequisite to such change is that management and staff share a common vision of where they want to bring their service. A fundamental shift in thinking cannot occur if social workers are constantly looking over their shoulder, and if managers revert to type at the slightest whiff of risk. One of the great hallmarks of a good manager is the holding of one's nerve when the going gets tough.

Yet, Spratt (2001), citing Giddens (1984), argues that while professional autonomy can be restricted by organisational constraints, individuals still possess a degree of power which they can use to effect change. The shift from the inquisitorial approach of child protection to the more partnership approach of family support requires social workers to relinquish a degree of power that traditionally came with the territory in child protection work. A simple example of this is the use of family group conferencing, or family welfare conferencing as it is known in Ireland. This methodology presented challenges to 'professional power, value systems and organisational expectations' where social workers had to divest themselves of their traditional roles, switching 'from decision maker to facilitator and enabler' (Morris and Tunnard, 1996). There is evidence that not all social workers are ready or willing to make this shift. For example, in Ireland, there was a relatively low usage of family welfare conferencing in the greater Dublin area, compared to the rest of the country (HSE, 2005).

The reluctance by practitioners to work with families in this way 'suggests that the 'hearts and minds' of professionals have not yet been won in relation to the model and its core values' (Browne, 2000). Like the proverbial light bulb, social workers have to really want to change. Therefore, it is a management responsibility to lead the change process by guiding staff into new and exciting territory and, by holding the risk at corporate level, allowing social workers to intervene in more creative ways without fear of failure or rebuke. Falling numbers of child protection cases should be seen as a cause for celebration, not concern, by managers. Social workers cannot make the significant shift from child protection to family support without the support of senior management and clear procedural guidance (NCH Action for Children, 1996).

Main Messages

- Early intervention will be more effective when it is in response to clear evidence of need and designed to address the causes of the problems being experienced.
- A management principle should be to provide a range of services targeted at different levels of need.
- To measure successful outcomes, describe how you are doing, not what you are doing.
- Moving from risk to well-being requires long-term changes in organisational and professional cultures.
- Staff need to be mandated by management to behave in a different way than before.

CHAPTER 4

Managing the child protection system

Defining and categorising child abuse

Not all children who require protection have been abused; and not all abused children require protection. Therefore, from the outset, in order to manage child protection services effectively, clarity is required regarding the basic concepts of abuse and protection. As has been evidenced in Chapter 1, there is a socio-political context for the framing of what is understood by abuse. Further, like society itself, it is not frozen in time but is in a constant state of evolution. Corby describes the notion of child abuse and neglect as 'highly contended concepts underpinned by and subject to a range of political and cultural factors particular to the society in which they occur' (Corby, 2006). In addition, the seminal work of Giovannoni and Becerra (1979) describe how child abuse and neglect is defined ultimately depends on 'value decisions', most especially those of the professionals involved in this area of work. Like beauty, it is in the eye of the beholder.

Sociology and anthropology will testify to the fact that no society is tolerant of child abuse within its ranks. Yet each society will define its own perimeters as to what exactly constitutes abuse. Because of societal differences there is not, and perhaps cannot be, a 'one size fits all' definition of child abuse and neglect. A global approach to child abuse must take into account differing expectations of parental behaviour in the context of a range of world-wide cultures. Culture has been defined as 'society's common fund of beliefs and behaviours, and its concepts of how people should conduct themselves' (WHO, 2002). Necessarily, any attempt to develop a universal definition of abuse must take cognisance of this cultural diversity; yet, by so doing, it is likely to be so all-embracing that it will become 'all things to all men'. The following is one such definition developed by the World Health Organisation:

> *Child abuse or maltreatment constitutes all forms of physical and/or emotional ill-treatment, sexual abuse, neglect or negligent treatment or commercial or other exploitation, resulting in actual or potential harm to the child's health, survival, development or dignity in the context of a relationship of responsibility, trust or power.*
>
> (WHO, 1999)

There is virtual universal agreement that sexual or physical abuse constitutes child maltreatment. Other behaviours such as child homelessness, child prostitution, abuse in out of home care and parental abandonment are also generally agreed to be abusive.

Yet, as has been evidenced by a survey of seventy-two countries undertaken by the International Society for the Prevention of Child Abuse, regional variation occurs with an unwillingness by some to label behaviours such as failure to secure medical care on religious grounds, physical discipline and female circumcision (ISPCAN, 2006).

Female circumcision is a pertinent example of how societal norms can, not only be different, but can actually be polarised. What is considered to be a cultural necessity in one country is considered to be genital mutualisation in another. For example, the practice which is widespread across socio-economic and religious groupings in over twenty-five African countries is outlawed in the United Kingdom under the *Female Genital Mutilation Act 2003*. There can be no ethical defence for preserving a practice that damages women's health and interferes with their sexuality. Yet it behoves those who are alien to the culture to at least familiarise themselves with the reasons for such cultural practices and to relate them to gender roles in their own society (Toubia, 1994).

Indeed, with the recent influx of people to these shores from a diverse range of national, religious and cultural backgrounds, the issue of non-medical male circumcision, so long an uncontested practice in the indigenous Jewish community, has also been now raised as an ethical and clinical dilemma among health professionals (HSE, 2007). There is a thin ethical line between prophylaxis and child abuse when the surgical benefits do not outweigh the harm caused (Benatar, 2006).

Ultimately the law of the land will be the final determinant as to what behaviour is right and what is wrong. Yet, as Giovannoni (1998) points out, statutes, although drawn up at different times for different purposes share one thing in common: they are vague. This being so, there is a judgement call to be made in interpreting the nuances of adult behaviour and assessing it against legal and cultural norms. Parton asserts that while there is general agreement that child abuse is a problem that something should be done about, there is less clarity about the nature of the problem, what should be done about it and how it should be done. In this context he contends that there has been a shift in the relationships and hierarchy of authority in key areas of decision making. While child abuse was constituted as a medico-social problem in the 1990s, it has shifted to a more socio-legal position nowadays where legal opinion dominates (Parton, 2002).

In this regard there is a job to be done by managers in order to avoid a tick-box culture, dominated by protocols and computer software, to nurture professional judgement among staff rather than having it stifled by others. Otherwise there is a risk that staff will go into a professional torpor, succumbing to the 'blame culture' and afraid to put their head above the parapet lest it is lopped off by those in authority, or by external forces including politicians, the media and public opinion. Creativity and professional, evidence-based, decision-making must be rewarded with senior management holding its corporate nerve to allow staff to do the thing they were hired to do: the application of individual, professional judgement.

Social services must occupy the vast grey area between medical and legal opinion and make it its own. For it is in that space that judgements and moral choices are made regarding what is culturally acceptable and what is socially, physically or mentally harmful;

what behaviour is normative and what is deviant and, most especially, to hear or represent the child's voice in determining what is in the best interest of the child, notwithstanding medical, legal or parental opinion.

Managers too are not immune to inertia. The underdevelopment of management roles has been identified as a key feature of systems failure in child protection services (McGuinness, 1993). As a consequence of this, it has been argued (Ferguson and O'Reilly, 2001) that the area is becoming much more bureaucratised and managed, with further layers of management being introduced. However the introduction of additional management functions is not, in itself a bad thing; it is how they are deployed that matters. If they contribute to producing safer practice and better outcomes for families, this can only be a good thing.

In the wake of the Baby P tragedy in Haringey, the Government has taken the decision to provide intensive training for children's service chiefs in order to strengthen leadership and management. Furthermore, it has been argued (Jones, 2009) that, in the UK, the merger of education and children's social care has meant that, increasingly, senior managers are coming from the educational sector and have little experience of sharp-end child protection. Jones (2009) argues that a short training course will not rectify matters and that senior managers with hands-on experience of child protection, need to occupy such senior posts. It is about getting the balance right.

With regard to balance, Parton (1998) describes a vision of society, where government is based on the exercise of freedom and where the relationship between liberty and discipline, freedom and rule, should be subject to continual re-negotiation. This must be so for, as we have seen, societal norms are not static and new, dynamic, issues will continuously emerge to challenge practitioners, managers and policy makers alike. For example, domestic servitude and sex slavery are relatively new additions to the spectrum of abuse. Managers must keep abreast of these emerging issues and to benchmark them against what is considered to be culturally appropriate, ethically sound and legal. Social services have no business intervening, uninvited, in the lives of families unless these conditions have been breached. In this regard the principle of subsidiarity comes into play.

Subsidiarity

John Stuart Mill, in his acclaimed essay On Liberty, expounds the view:

That the only purpose for which power can be rightfully exercised over any member of a civilised community, against his will, is to prevent harm to others. His own good, either physical or moral, is not a sufficient warrant. He cannot rightfully be compelled to do or forbear because it will be better for him to do so, because it will make him happier, because, in the opinions of others, to do so would be wise, or even right. These are good reasons for remonstrating with him, or reasoning with him, or persuading him, or entreating him, but not for compelling him, or visiting him with any evil in case he do otherwise.

(Mill, 1869)

Therein lays the moral mandate for state intervention: the prevention of harm to others.
    A key principle of subsidiarity is the belief that nothing should be done by a larger, more complex organisation that can reasonably be done by a smaller, simpler, organisation. The principle is the bulwark of limited government and personal freedom. As such it is diametrically opposed to bureaucracy and centralisation, which have been described as characteristic of the Welfare State (Bosnich, 1996).
    In the aftermath of the Second World War fresh social thinking began to emerge in Britain. War had a levelling effect on British society. As Fraser put it, 'Bombs, unlike unemployment, knew no social distinctions' (Fraser, 1984). The Government commissioned the *Beveridge Report*, which proposed a radical insurance scheme offering, in return for contributions, benefits at an adequate level, payable as of right without means testing. This was the stepping stone to the creation of the Welfare State. Legislation quickly followed governing universal cover and security for individuals through family allowance payments, national insurance, national assistance and compensation for industrial accidents.
    The mood in Ireland at the same time could not have been more different. It prompted the Rev. Prof. Cornelius Lucy, later to become Catholic Bishop of Cork, to write: 'there should be little question of adopting the Beveridge Report here in detail or indeed in principle' (Lucy, 1943). There was a series of notorious clashes between the Irish Government and the Catholic Church while the former attempted advance health and social reform. Most notable was the *Mother and Child Scheme* which, in the wake of high tuberculosis-related deaths and high infant mortality rates, sought to introduce free maternity services and free medical services to children up to the age of sixteen years. The Catholic hierarchy declared the scheme to be contrary to Catholic social teaching resulting, after heated public debate, in the resignation of the Minister of Health who proposed it.
    Opposition was also mounted to the introduction of the first adoption legislation in the early 1950s for fear that would facilitate proselytism and in the belief that it was fundamentally unchristian to deprive a natural mother irrevocably of her rights over her child. In fact, as Whyte described it;' . . . there was a whole bevy of interlocking groups . . . dedicated to reshaping Ireland on the lines laid down by the Catholic social principles' (Whyte, 1980).
    These attitudes and behaviour, while serving as a further example of shifting social morality, provide the genesis of another, more palatable, principle that is embedded in contemporary best practice: the principle of minimum intervention. According to it, services should not be imposed unless their purpose is the avoidance of harm.

Getting the balance right

There is no doubt that public scrutiny, brought about by successive inquiries into child abuse cases has put 'the frighteners 'on managers and practitioners alike.
    There is a high public expectation that, not only will cases be acted upon, but that they will be detected in time. Currently in Ireland, a yet unpublished report is awaited into the

deaths of a father, mother and two children in Monageer, County Wexford, where initial reports suggest that the family were previously unknown to child protection services. Without pre-empting the results of the inquiry into Monageer, this nevertheless raises the question as to how services might be expected to respond to situations that were unpredictable.

The sad reality is that child protection workers will never be able to protect all children from abuse. Yet, according to Ferguson (2004), the paradox is that the better social workers get at protecting children the greater is the public and political outcry when they fail to do so.

An unintended consequence of this is that it has led to very defensive practice. This in turn can lead to inappropriate interference into family life. It can also have the effect of diluting the concentration on priority cases and can also divert resources and attention away from welfare services (Freeman, 1996). Spratt (2000) argues that, in a culture of blame, practitioners tend to respond to low risk cases in the same way as if significant child protection concerns were present. As well as defensive practice, inadequate resources, a lack of focus on preventative work and limited use of a wide range of alternative orders are also used to explain an increase in the number of care applications in England and Wales (McGhee and Francis, 2003).

These factors result in a situation where there is, at worst, a lingering inertia or, at best, an ongoing ambivalence towards adopting a welfare model of intervention, even in cases where this is entirely appropriate. Freeman (1996) rightly asserts that managing child abuse cannot be reduced to the social work equivalent of 'painting by numbers' as there will always be the requirement for the application of judgement based on as comprehensive an assessment of each case as possible. She goes on to argue that child abuse involves two elements: significant harm and familial responsibility for that harm. She also makes an essential assertion that where little harm is done, either physically or psychologically, it should not be classified as child abuse, even if the family is entirely responsible for the harm done. Similarly, if there has been major harm caused but the family were only responsible in a minor way, this should not be classified as child abuse either (Freeman, 1996).

Statistical analysis supports the argument that there can be over-zealousness when practice is stuck in a child protection rut. By way of example, an analysis undertaken in Australia showed that notifications and recalculations of child abuse and neglect during the period 2003–2004 revealed that three-quarters of the cases were not substantiated. For many families who were subject of a notification, there was little evidence to justify such action in the first place (Ainsworth and Hansen, 2006). According to Ainsworth and Hansen (2006) the child protection surveillance net is catching 'well meaning but imperfect parents' who are being victimised, rather than helped, by the system.

In England there is evidence that, over the ten years between 1996 and 2006 there has been no appreciable reduction in the numbers of children being registered, despite the aspirations of government policy and a plethora of procedures and guidance (DfES, 2006).

On the other hand, registering a child as being at risk is no guarantee of their safety. For example, in the cases of Baby P in Haringey and Shannon Mathews in Kirkess, both had been placed on the child protection register.

There will always be the dilemma of avoiding unwarranted intrusion on the one hand and being criticised for failing to protect children on the other (Parton and Mathews, 2001). The challenge is to manage that uncertainty in the knowledge that one may never have the full picture regarding any particular family.

Another factor is the philosophy, prevalent within child protection work, that 'volume is good'. Numbers of child abuse referrals are often used as a validation for the existence of a service or as barter for additional resources. Commenting on the history and development of child protection work, Ferguson (2004) noted that the National Society for the Prevention of Cruelty to Children, in early reports, used statistics on child deaths to assert the value of its work. Rather than have history repeat itself, a better measure of success ought to be a reduction in the numbers of cases being categorised as child abuse.

A core value of social work practice is to work alongside service users and practitioners in a participative approach to planning and implementing change. An important feature of social work practice is the value attached to human relationships and the principles and values that underpin practice. Social care managers operate in a political environment that is subject to legal requirements, statutory controls and procedures and standards and performance is not as clear cut as in 'for profit 'organisations. Therefore, the manager's role is predominated by balancing, the oft times conflicting, demands of the organisation (Johnson and Williams, 2007).

In essence managers need to:
- Embrace the legal and policy mandate.
- Set out the vision at organisational level.
- Reconfigure services and re-balance budgets as needs be.
- Accept responsibility for the consequences of doing things differently.
- Support staff through the change process and beyond.
- Carry corporate responsibility for the consequences in practice of the policy shift.
- Promote evidence-based practice.
- Ensure that consistent quality standards are upheld.

As has been detailed in Chapter 3 there is nothing particularly new about the refocusing debate and the structuring of children's services in ways that seek to achieve a better balance between earlier intervention and protection. However, with regard to fresh thinking there is a movement, which started in the USA, that began to question the forensic nature of child protection work. Thinking developed whereby, instead of providing either a child protection service or a child welfare service, a model emerged which combined the two approaches. While prioritising the safety of the child, services were simultaneously offered which focused on family strengths. This dual approach became known as the Differential Response Model. While it cannot claim to be a 'new invention', or a unique methodology, it does offer a softer alternative to the traditional approach to child protection. As such, it warrants some consideration, not just as a practice initiative, but for the opportunities it provides managers for creative resource deployment.

Differential response model

The Differential Response Model (DRM) allows child protection services to respond in a different way to cases of child abuse and neglect. It moves away from the traditional investigative approach and takes a twin-track approach which, while remaining focused on child safety, takes a strengths-based approach that focuses on the family as a whole.

It is a feature in many jurisdictions that many cases are screened out at the point of entry to the child protection system because they were not considered to have met the threshold of severity deemed necessary to receive a service. As a result many families referred for a service do not receive one, even though the children may be vulnerable. Often, no alternative service is provided. As a consequence many of these families are re-referred at a later stage, often when their problems have become more acute. However, DRM seeks to intervene in low to moderate risk cases, seeking to intervene earlier in order to restore family equilibrium by promoting family welfare rather than responding to any particular episode or event (Harrison, 2007).

A number of trends have been identified that are present in child protection systems in a number of jurisdictions, including the United Kingdom and Ireland (Buckley, 2007):

- Responses to concerns tended to focus on incidents and on fault finding.
- At the same time child protection cases continue to increase but often did not meet the threshold to receive a service and were closed.
- Other cases were closed soon after the immediate safety concerns were addressed and no attempt was made to address underlying complex family problems.
- There was a high rate of re-referral, often after problems has escalated.
- Child protection services dominated, with family support services being grafted on to them, rather than being an integral part of the overall system.
- Public perception of statutory child care services was negative.
- There was a growing acknowledgement of the value of promoting protective behaviours.
- There was a need for more measurable outcomes.

For many of these reasons New Zealand embraced the Differential Response Model in 2005. In addition to increasing numbers of child abuse and neglect notifications, there was also an increasing number of children coming into care. The Ministry of Social Development (Child, Youth and Families) made a conscious shift from a transactional approach to one that was outcome-focused. The transactional approach was event driven with a focus on 'front-end' activity such as notifications and getting families through the system. Management effort went into avoiding system failure by emphasising compliance, increased documentation and 'information fiefdoms' (Connolly, 2007). By contrast the outcome-focused approach is based on need, focusing on continuity and stability. It relies upon relationship development and change, with a flexible response aligned to need (Connolly, 2007).

DRM does not obsess about categorising cases into forms of abuse or neglect; nor does it worry unduly as to whether abuse is confirmed or not. Instead it makes the assumption that most parents want to do the best for their children, even though personal or family difficulties may be impeding them. Therefore, DRM focuses not only on protecting children from harm, but also on improving child and family well-being by improving child functioning and strengthening the family's capacity to cope.

Another feature of DRM is that it relies heavily upon community and non-statutory organisations. Instead of these agencies passing risky cases to the statutory sector like the proverbial hot potato, they are encouraged to remain involved and to take a key worker role where appropriate.

DRM was introduced into Ontario, Canada, in 2007. This followed a fundamental review of child protection practice and a change of legislation, the primary purpose of which was that there should be 'the least disruptive acts' to protect a child (Marshall, Hallberg and Reid, 2007). New Child Protection Standards have been introduced that set out the goals of the Differential Response Model of the Child Protection Service:

- To maintain a strong focus on child safety, well-being and permanence.
- To provide more case-sensitive, customised responses for referrals of non-severe situations.
- To strengthen assessment and decision-making by implementing a family-centred team decision-making model, 'next generation' clinical tools and specialised supplementary screening tools.
- To increase the use of clinical tools with a broader clinical focus.
- To increase the emphasis on engaging children and families in the service.
- To build on existing strengths and increase families' capacity.
- To involve a wider range of informal and formal supports in services planning and provision.

(Ministry of Children and Youth Services, Ontario, 2007)

The model supports two approaches to investigation. The 'traditional' model continues to be used in cases where a criminal assault has been made against a child, or in other extremely severe cases. All other lower risk cases employ a 'customised 'model that adopts a more collaborative approach. This so-called customised approach provides child protection workers with a more flexible range of options that are tailored to meet the unique needs of children and families while ensuring the safety of the child. The model emphasises a strengths-based approach to services delivery and actively encourages the engagement of children, families and their support systems in decision-making and service planning (Ministry of Children and Youth Services, Ontario, 2007).

In jurisdictions where DRM has been tried and tested, the benefits are generally found to be the same and can be summarised as follows:

- child safety remains uncompromised
- there were fewer reports of maltreatment
- families liked the approach
- social workers supported it
- it cost less in the long term
- there were fewer investigations
- there were less repeat referrals
- fewer children came into care
- the courts became less involved
- there was more family involvement
- more children were served

(Harrison, 2007)

The use of DRM is not intended to alter the threshold at which referrals are screened in, but it will provide more options based on need and not just on safety and risk. It does this by focusing on the needs of children and families and upon the services that are required to promote and restore family welfare, without having to sift through information in order to establish whether a particular incident occurred or not (Buckley, 2007). While urgent protective responses will continue to be a priority, there is a growing interest in developing alternative responses that are tailored to meeting the diverse needs of maltreated children and by supporting more collaboration with non-statutory service providers and community supports (Trocmé, Knott and Knoke, 2003).

Protecting the right children

Even services that are entirely committed to Differential Response accept that some cases are going to require what Little and Mount (1999) dubbed as 'heavy end' services aimed at remedying serious difficulties, as has been seen in the Ontario approach above. Senior managers need to have systems in place that can provide them with the simple assurance that the right children are getting the right service at the right time. The *Climbié Inquiry Report* (2003) made a landmark finding that there was 'a gross failure of the system' in that case (1.18) and it identified senior managers, as well as practitioners, as responsible for this.

Unfortunately, five years on, similar conclusions were drawn in the case of Baby P in Haringey. While in Doncaster, the Department of Children, Schools and Families is inquiring into the Council's management capacity following the deaths of a number of children in its area. In Ireland, the Ombudsman for Children has announced that her Office is to carry out an investigation to establish if there has been any maladministration in relation to the handling of the Child Protection Audit of Catholic Church Dioceses by the Health Services Executive and/or the Department of Health. Clearly, there is currently much public scrutiny of the way the child protection system is managed.

The child protection system

Case workers will manage the cases, supervisors will manage the caseworkers, but managers must manage the system. It is not a function that can be left to others or, indeed, to chance.

Referring to the system in the UK, Masson (1997) expresses concern about existing child protection systems in that resources are being expended on the investigation of cases but identified needs are still not being met. Only a minority of cases that are the subject of investigations actually receive a service. The second Joint Chief Inspectors Report (2005) provides more recent support for this contention. It stated that some agencies are still not giving sufficient priority to safeguarding children's interests and that there were still small groups of vulnerable children that were not being given sufficient recognition or priority. It also highlighted differing thresholds in child protection and family support and stated that 'children are not uniformly receiving the care and protection they need . . .' (4.53).

The report, *Making Social Care Better for People* (CSCI, 2005) brought together evidence from inspections of children's social services in almost half of all English local councils. It concluded that as more resources were being directed towards increasingly intensive assessment processes, they were not always available to fund personalised help for children and families. It also noted that few councils were able to change their practice in order to reduce the numbers of children requiring child protection services and care proceedings. Further, it noted that neighbouring councils often had very different rates of child protection registrations and numbers of children in care. This was attributed to 'the very different organisational cultures, leadership styles and the varying emphasis given to performance management and quality assurance' (2.31).

The most approximate comparator in the Irish context is the Social Service Inspectorate report on the monitoring of the implementation of new national guidelines on child protection and welfare (SSI, 2003). While praising the fact that a national strategy was adopted to implement these guidelines, it did express concern that a new Child Protection Notification System was being implemented in different ways in different parts of the country: 'A truly national approach to policy implementation can only be achieved if each health board relinquishes its discretion to do things its own way' (SSI, 2003). There needs to be a level of consistency across jurisdictions if service users are to have an equitable experience of the service.

Masson (1997) suggests criteria against which any system to protect children should be benchmarked:

- It should have clear duties to those in need of protection.
- Those providing the service should be accountable to the community.
- The service should be professionally competent and recognised as such.
- It should provide a safety level which is acceptable to the community generally and to children.
- It must satisfy existing standards of justice.

Echoing the sentiments of *Making Social Care Better for People* (2005), the consistent presence of such criteria in a child protection system requires an appropriate organisational culture, positive leadership and a robust system of performance management and quality assurance.

An under-recognised or -acknowledged feature of a child protection system is the fact that assessments and decisions often have to be made with information that is incomplete. According to Munro (1996) identifying child abuse and assessing risk is more like making a jigsaw than a process of observation. Fragments of information must be gathered and fitted together to form an overall picture of a family. Judgements have to be made with knowledge that is less than perfect and will therefore require review and revision as more information becomes available.

Munro (1996) highlights research which shows that social workers are persistently slow to change their minds in the light of new information. For this reason she agues that, paradoxically, making mistakes in child protection can be a sign of good practice in that it demonstrates an ability to be self-critical with the ability to change one's mind. This being so, the management task in a child protection system is to gather together available knowledge, external standards, organisational procedures and statutory requirements so that they form an integrated support to both the individual and practice as a whole (Kearney, 2004).

Key factors linked to vulnerability

Prevalence

Child protection systems in themselves are not tools to measure the prevalence or incidence of child abuse and protection *per se*. They are, in effect, a system to manage known cases. For example, the child protection register has been described as a central record to ensure that child protection plans are regularly reviewed (Gibbons *et al.*, 1995). In Ireland there is not an actual child protection register. However, the Child Protection Notification System, prescribed in *Children First*, the national guidelines for child protection and welfare (DoH&C, 1999), essentially fulfils the same function in that it is a record of reported cases where the progress of each is monitored until there is a final outcome.

Yet the question has been asked (Pugh, 2007): if such systems cannot be taken as an account of the extent of abuse or risk, what do they tell us? In terms of prevalence, while they may represent a reasonable indication of children who are at risk and have come to official attention, there is no way of knowing the numbers of children who are at risk and have not. In addition there is strong evidence to indicate that variations occur regarding which children do and do not come under surveillance (Joint Chief Inspectors Report, 2005; Pugh, 2007). There are several operational factors that might account for such variations:

• Local perceptions of what constitutes significant harm.
• Local variations regarding how quickly cases are reviewed and ultimately removed from the system.

- The extent to which policies and procedures are effective in diverting children out of formal systems in less formal interventions.
- The availability of such less formal interventions.

(Pugh, 2007)

Again, this highlights the need for national standardisation and consistency of approach.

Socio-economic factors

There is also evidence to show that socio-economic factors have an influence on which children come to the attention of the authorities. For example, links have been found between unemployment, stress, poverty and child abuse (Little and Gibbons, 1993; Gordon and Gibbons, 1998).Similarly, in a study undertaken in Northern Ireland (Winter and Connolly, 2005), a strong association was found between the number of referrals received from a particular area and the level of deprivation within it. Winter and Connolly (2005) suggest the promotion of a 'structuralist approach', which seeks to locate child abuse in the broader context and which addresses the relationship between social structural factors and child abuse. Their study highlights a very important conclusion that, given the strong relationship between levels of deprivation and rates of referrals, there are serious limitations in relying upon what they describe as 'individualistic explanations of child abuse'.

Adverse personal circumstances and child protection

In Ireland, Public Health Nurses have a statutory obligation to visit all newborn babies within the first few days of their arrival home and to conduct ongoing developmental checks until the child is at least three years old. This provides an excellent universal radar with which to identify problems at an early stage. Yet a common frustration among Public Health Nurses is that when they identify a child in significant need, it still may not be enough to reach the threshold to elicit a response from the child protection social workers.

In Swords, a rapidly growing town in north county Dublin, a study was undertaken that profiled the needs of children living in this area who were identified by Public Health Nurses as having unmet social needs (NAHB, 2002).

Among the sample as a whole, twenty-nine per cent of children lived in overcrowded accommodation, thirty-four per cent were considered to be living in a poor neighbourhood, thirty-five per cent were socially isolated, fifty-five per cent were living on incomes from the state, and twenty-four per cent of the children displayed behavioural problems. Not surprisingly, therefore, in three-quarters of the cases the carers were considered to be overburdened, with forty-three per cent of them suffering from some form of depression.

In overall terms the study revealed that there were constellations of need among the children, not just single factors. The most common finding, in twenty-six per cent of cases, was the need for improved psychological child health, together with better parent-child relationship; with a further twenty-four per cent needing alleviation of adult depression and improved family relationships. Clearly the needs of the parents, if unaddressed, will adversely affect the health and well-being of the child. Furthermore, most families had a multitude of problems that did not neatly fit into the remit of a single agency.

Implications for management

All of this has clear implications for the management of child protection services. While child protection systems themselves provide a useful means of monitoring and managing cases within the system, there is a necessity for managers to proactively consider how all children requiring protection receive it. For example, under the Irish *Child Care Act* 1991 there is an onus on the authorities to: 'take such steps as it considers requisite to identify children who are not receiving adequate care and protection . . . in its area' (3) (2)a. This duty, although not elaborated upon in statute, policy or guidance, remains an obligation on services not just to sit back and take what comes in the door like a local corner shop, but to go out and find it.

The linkages between socio-economic factors and the prevalence of referrals from deprived areas make a strong argument for services not to rely solely upon individual reports of abuse. Managers need to consider the needs of whole communities and ways in which the strengths of neighbourhoods and communities can be harnessed. People in local communities are safeguarding children all the time by simple neighbourly acts such as looking out for a neighbour's child or campaigning for safer streets. There are many ways in which those who plan and manage services can link more formally organised services to local initiatives and can help to support and expand these informal activities to really make a difference in protecting children (Gill and Jack, 2007). This concept, which is heretofore underdeveloped in child protection services, is expanded upon in Chapter 7.

Similarly, where social deprivation is prominent within families it is not enough to consider the needs of children in isolation from the parents and the family as a whole. As in the case of the Swords study above, if the primary carer is poor, isolated and depressed, their capacity to raise the health and well-being of their child will be greatly diminished. Typically child protection services tend to tackle the issue that is causing the immediate risk and then withdraw without addressing the underlying difficulties of the carer or the overall needs of the family. In the study undertaken by Pugh (2005) it was noted that one local authority that made a concerted effort at refocusing its services towards child welfare had proportionately fewer children on the register. Similar findings were observed elsewhere (Oliver *et al.*, 2001: Greenfields and Statham, 2004). Also, because broader health and social problems within a family do not fit conveniently under the auspices of any one agency, there is an onus on child protection service managers to forge alliances with related services and to devise strategies to tackle family problems on a number of fronts; not just single child protection episodes that may have prompted the original referral.

The neglect of Neglect

In the nineteen-sixties physical abuse was placed firmly on the agenda by Henry Kempe when he wrote *The Battered Baby Syndrome* (Kempe, 1962). The seeking out of so-called non-accidental injury became a major preoccupation of child protection services for the next two decades. This was superceded in the early 1980s with the dawning awareness among professionals of the phenomenon of child sexual abuse. For whatever reason, sexual abuse became a 'super specialism'. For example in Dublin, as early as 1988, two hospital-based sexual abuse assessment units were established, headed by consultant psychiatrists. Sexual abuse was put on a medico-legal pedestal whereby, in the few cases that ever got to court, medical evidence was favoured by lawyers and judges alike. However, social workers were acceptable for any other form of child maltreatment requiring assessment or presentation in court.

In Ireland in 2004, forty-two per cent of cases referred to the Child Protection Notification System were neglect, making it the most notified type of concern (DoH&C, 2006). The exact same trend applies to England where neglect accounted for forty-three per cent of cases referred to child protection registers (DfES, 2006). This may be attributable to the fact that child protection systems are largely attuned to dealing with episodic events or incidents, or that the preferred response of child protection systems is along procedural and predictable lines. As a result they tend to deal with the consequences of an incident of neglect, with the causes or the insidious effects of persistent, on going, neglect remaining hidden under the child protection radar.

A study undertaken in one Irish health board area (Horwath and Bishop, 2001) found that, although neglect accounted for more than half of the cases reported, there was nevertheless a lack of common understanding among staff as to the precise meaning of child neglect. Forty-one per cent of professional respondents believed that social workers accepted lower standards of parenting than other professionals. Yet, just over twelve per cent of those same respondents used the same criteria for assessing clients as they would for themselves or friends. Clearly, there is a level of ambivalence regarding what constitutes neglect.

According to Iwaniec (1995), neglect can be described as 'hostile or indifferent parental behaviour which damages a child's self-esteem, degrades a sense of achievement, diminishes a sense of belonging and stands in the way of health and vigorous and happy development. 'It is more common, lasts longer and usually has longer-term effects than other forms of abuse (Berry, Charlson and Dawson, 2003). A distinction can be made between reactive neglect that can be episodic in nature, and chronic neglect that is long-term in nature, yet service provision is primarily focused on other forms of abuse (Tanner and Turney, 2003). For this reason, and because of the disposition of services to respond to episodic events, it is reasonable to conclude that it is mainly reactive neglect that is picked up by the child protection system with the on-going, unrelenting and chronic cases going largely unnoticed or not responded to.

Reflecting the above discussion on socio-economic and personal disadvantage, patterns of abuse and neglect have been identified as being influenced by very different factors. These differences include structural elements such as poverty and unemployment, family stress, social isolation, single parenthood and parental mental illness and substance abuse (Berry, Charlson and Dawson, 2003).

A study undertaken in Dublin (Harrison, 2003) showed that one health board area had much fewer reported cases of neglect than the national average. Forty-two per cent of reports concerned sexual abuse with neglect accounting for just twenty-five per cent, against a national average of forty per cent for the same period. Yet it emerged that neglect was the primary reason for children being received into care in that health board area. The study revealed that although sexual, physical and emotional abuse combined, accounted for seventy-five per cent of all reported cases of child abuse, they accounted for only nine per cent of all admissions to care. Conversely, while neglect accounted for only twenty-five per cent of all reported cases of abuse it accounted for thirty-four per cent of all the children in care. This clearly indicated the need to focus interventions more sharply upon the issue of neglect in order to prevent family breakdown and reduce the numbers of children coming into care for this reason. Instead of dealing with neglect on a case by case basis, an overall intervention strategy was required to alleviate the disproportionately adverse effects of neglect.

Work undertaken in the United States of America suggests that particular techniques may offer better outcomes in cases of child neglect (Berry, Charlson and Dawson, 2003):

- Family-centred child welfare work recognises that child well-being is intrinsically linked to the welfare of the family as a whole.
- As maternal depression is a primary contributor to child neglect, this must be addressed if the mother's ability to parent is to be enhanced.
- Acknowledging that 'substance abuser' is just one aspect of a person's identity can be the basis of forming alliances with related services for the benefit of the family as a whole.
- Meeting the immediate needs of families includes broader environmental disadvantage.
- From an eco-behavioural perspective in-home services are more effective in that families are more comfortable and open to learning and sharing.

Main Messages

- Not all children who require protection have been abused and not all abused children require protection.
- A measure of success ought to be a reduction in the numbers of child abuse cases, not the volume of such cases.
- Differential responses focus on need and what is required to restore family welfare and equilibrium, rather than on whether a particular incident occurred or not.
- Managers must ensure consistency of approach across teams and service units if the service user is to have an equitable experience of the service.
- In identifying abuse and assessing risk, judgements must be made with knowledge that is less than perfect.
- Linkages between socio-economic factors and prevalence of referrals make a strong argument for services to address the relationship between social structural factors and child abuse.
- The insidious and longer-term effects of neglect require greater attention from service providers.

CHAPTER 5

Managing to protect children from and in care

Definitions and scope

The terminology for describing children in care varies from country to country and indeed from setting to setting. Descriptions such as children in care, looked after children, substitute care and alternative care all more or less mean the same thing but are subject to local preference. Ultimately it is legislation that prescribes precisely what is meant by the terms. In the United Kingdom the term 'looked after' refers to children who are the subject of care orders or interim care orders under Sections 31 and 38 of the *Child Care Act 1989* and those who are in voluntary care, accommodated by the local authority under Sections 20 and 21. In Ireland children may be placed in voluntary care under Section 4 of the *Child Care Act 1991* or on foot of interim care orders or care orders under Sections 17 and 18 respectively. In addition, both jurisdictions have emergency legislative provisions.

The term 'accommodation' requires some further explanation. Under the 1989 Act accommodation broadly equates to voluntary care; although it may also include children who are on remand or under police protection who, no doubt, would not describe themselves as being in 'voluntary' care. As expounded by Packman and Hall (1998) there are degrees of 'voluntariness'. Furthermore, it is probably fair to say that some parents agree to voluntary care because they were made an offer that they could not refuse; in other words, an implicit threat of court action if they did not comply with the voluntary arrangements proposed. The 1991 Act, under Section 5, makes a curious provision for children who are homeless, allowing them to be placed in 'suitable accommodation' without recourse to voluntary or statutory care. In any event, for the purpose of this narrative, the term 'children in care' refers to all children in either the voluntary or statutory care of the state.

Protecting children from care

Avoidance of care

There are few so foolish as to think that a child who is placed in care is automatically destined for a life to be lived happily ever after. Because of the pervasiveness of change in the child's life, Kadushin (1985) argues that care should be regarded as 'the third line of defence' and that every effort must be made to keep the home intact for the child and to keep the child in the home. As has been seen with welfare and protection in earlier chapters, it has long since been recognised that there is predictability as to which families are at risk of breaking up.

As early as the 1960s Dinnage and Kellmer Pringle (1965) identified as being at risk those families with low incomes and more than four children, one-parent families, those suffering from serious or chronic physical or mental illness or disability and those affected by sudden disaster or a disrupting crisis. They suggest that such predictability should make prevention possible. Similarly, the point has been made long ago that most of these families are known to social workers, yet the crisis precipitating admission to care often takes the social workers by surprise. This raises concerns regarding the levels of preventative work and what has been described as a 'paucity of contingency planning' (Millham *et al.*, 1986). It also begs the question as to why other community-based alternatives to care, such as day care, day foster care and supervision orders are not used more extensively. For example, in Ireland in 2006, of the 5,247 children in care only 193 (3.7 per cent) were described as being at home under a supervision order (HSE, 2006).

In Chapters 3 and 4 references have been made to the advantages of strengths-based approaches with families, ecological approaches and family centred work, which all serve to strengthen the family as a whole, and parents in particular. However, it is worth bearing in mind that a further line of defence can be direct work with children to build up their strengths and resilience. The resilience approach is optimistic and pragmatic. A resilient child is likely to have better outcomes than might be expected in their particular adverse circumstances (Gilligan, 2001). By reducing problems one by one from what Gilligan (2001) refers to as 'the stockpile of problems,' disproportionately advantageous results may be achieved with some children. Even if children are experiencing adverse home-life experiences it still may be possible for them to thrive in other areas of their life, thus developing overall self-reliance. In this regard professionals are urged to appreciate the protective value of positive school and spare time experiences (Gilligan, 2000; Gilligan, 1998; Sylva, 1994). Professionals should not wait until the child has entered the care system before they begin to strengthen their resilience: rather they should pay attention to the little things that might make all the difference in strengthening their immunity and resistance to adversity while they are still at home in order to avoid admission to care.

Adverse effects of care

Even a positive care experience is an adversity in the life of a child because they have already experienced the unfavourable effects of separation, loss and, possibly, harm. There is a considerable body of evidence to suggest that separating children from parents or other adult carers, and from familiar surroundings, can do them harm (Packman *et al.*, 1986). Furthermore, children who remain in long term care from an early age generally show higher incidences of emotional disturbance and poorer educational attainment.

Although the potential risk to children in care by adults has been given increased attention, the risk that children may experience from each other has received considerably less consideration. In a survey of children in care, there was no mechanism employed to ensure that the child would be a good match to the children already in placement. Furthermore, when the histories of sexually abused children in the study were examined, half of them abused another child at some stage, usually another child in care (Farmer and Pollock, 1999). Clearly, care, unless it is managed well, can be a toxic environment. Conversely it might be seen as a 'powerful medicine' deserving of careful consideration as to whether it is warranted and in what dose (length of stay) what expected benefits; and whether less invasive interventions might suffice (Rosenberg *et al.* 2007). This requires some consideration as to the purpose of care.

The appropriate use of care

It has been asserted (Packman *et al.*, 1986) that the real issue is not how to reduce numbers in care, but rather the nature and purpose of care and its appropriateness as a means of meeting the needs that gave rise to it. Packman and others (1986) go on to elaborate that care is not a 'unitary concept' and set out three primary reasons for admissions to care:
1. Requests for care where parents are seen as unfortunate and not blameworthy and the state acts as the child's caretaker on behalf of the parents.
2. The state provides protection and rescue for children who are considered to be in danger, whether it be physical, sexual, moral, emotional, or developmental.
3. Children whose behaviour is causing problems.

It is evident, therefore, that admission to care is a response to a range of problems. In Ireland in 2005 parental inability to cope accounted for twenty-five per cent of all children in care; protection from abuse and neglect accounted for thirty-eight per cent, and children's behavioural problems accounted for two-per cent (HSE, 2005).

These statistics clearly indicate that if more were done to assist parents to cope there would be fewer children in care, at a considerable saving to the state. This requires a senior management decision to re-direct resources towards interventions that are aimed strategically at parents who are struggling before they can no longer cope. As was demonstrated in Chapter 3, many parents are over-burdened by socio-economic and adverse personal circumstances that, if tackled early enough and comprehensively enough, could be abated.

With regard to children with behavioural difficulties, although the statistical information is not available, anecdotal evidence suggests that this two per cent represents older children who have become outside the control of their parents and, most likely their school and community as well. These are likely to be children and young people over thirteen years who are placed in residential care and, due to their challenging behaviour, are at high risk of placement breakdown. This is supported by a study that was conducted in Warwickshire (Cliffe, 1992) which showed that, of an overall placement breakdown of forty-per cent, young people over thirteen years were twice as likely to experience a breakdown in their placement.

Although, as a percentage, the children with behavioural problems is a small group, that two per cent in the Irish statistics represents one hundred and seven young people who entered the care system late and who are not likely to do well there. A high percentage of this cohort of young people goes on to become homeless, largely because their behaviour cannot be managed by the care system as well as the parents, the school and the communities. Many of them, as a consequence, end up in secure care or the juvenile justice system with a bleak long-term prognosis. Care, therefore, is of little or no assistance to these young people as the door was bolted long after the horse was gone. Therefore, the appropriateness of care ought to be borne in mind when decisions are being taken regarding the best ways of meeting such children's needs.

While advocating community based options, it would be an over statement to consider all out of home care as evidence of a failure of the system. It can and does provide an appropriate service to those children and young people who both need it and can avail of it. However, the purpose of this chapter is not to elaborate on the relative benefits of care but to advocate alternatives and to warn about possibly negative, or indeed, harmful effects of care.

Where care is deemed to be necessary, the setting needs to provide a homelike environment with the capacity to manage, nurture and heal. In the case of children with high-risk behaviours, this behaviour must be managed within a supportive environment that relies on positive reinforcement, positive relationships and personal growth rather than suppression and control. Hence, the concept of care should not be seen as a 'last resort' as last resorts are undesirable and unconstructive places to be (Packman et al., 1986). Where care is required it should be regarded as the right thing for the right child right now.

Decision-making and the role of management

Despite national policy aspirations, management strategies and practice initiatives, the trend for the numbers of children in care continues to hover between static and upward (DoH&C, 2006; HSE, 2006; Department for Innovation, Universities and Skills, 2007). Dickens et al. (2007) suggest that while the overall number of admissions has gone down, the average stay in care has increased and this is borne out by official statistics (DoH, 2003). However, what is striking is the variation between local authorities as featured in inspections and elsewhere (DoH, 2003; Adams, 2001).Why this should be so requires some explanation.

A number of possible factors have been suggested, including socio-demographic factors in particular areas, departmental policies and procedures, insufficient preventative services, staffing levels and resources, the culture of departments and the beliefs and attitude of individual staff (Dickens et al., 2007; Millham et al., 1986; Oliver et al., 2001; Statham et al., 2002). The linkages between socio-demographic factors have been discussed in Chapter 3, however, individual attitude and departmental culture require some further exploration.

Oliver *et al.* (2001) saw an association between high numbers in care and what they describe as 'an interventionist and legalistic approach' underpinned by an organisational ethos of caution. They stress that departmental culture is crucial, in effect highlighting the need for strong leadership if such a culture is to be altered. One of the basic characteristics of good management in the area of child protection is the holding of one's nerve. It is all too tempting to ward off any possibility of blame by taking the easy way out. However, if managers are to be successful in shifting the culture to allow for positive and controlled risk-taking they must 'carry the can' at corporate level for practitioners, absolving them of blame if a plan that has been agreed upon backfires.

Oliver *et al.* (2001) also saw an association between high numbers in care and a lack of strategic oversight and the under-developed family support services. Statham *et al.* (2001) stress the need for sufficient preventative services, consistent procedures for monitoring placement decisions and the requirement to have good recruitment and retention procedures to ensure motivated and well-trained staff.

Dickens *et al.* (2007), in a study, addressed at what level of management approval was given for a child to come into care. Critically, they discovered that in authorities with high admissions, decisions tended to be made at a relatively low level; whereas, in authorities with lowest admission rates, decisions tended to be made at a higher level. Again they stress that it is not just the management tier involved but the prevailing culture of the department. It is remarkable but true that in some social service departments junior decision-makers can decide to place a child in care for the duration of their childhood, with all that entails for the child and at considerable cost to the state; while the same person may have to seek permission from a higher authority to, for example, travel outside the catchment area. It speaks volumes about the values at play and clearly indicates the role management must play in defining organisational culture and the values that underpin them. Without an awareness of values, practice can become dangerous; it is not an optional extra but lies at the core of best practice (Moss, 2007).

There is a need for clear procedures regarding not only at what level decisions are made to admit children into care, but also the need to monitor placement decision-making. There is an obvious requirement for services to have strategies in place to deliberately attempt to avoid admissions to care by, as we have seen, targeted interventions at cohorts that are known to be vulnerable. Such strategies should also address the more flexible use of community care provisions, such as day fostering, and the more creative use of legal options, such as supervision orders.

Decision-making matrix for children in care

Dickens *et al.* (2007) devised a decision-making matrix that highlights various options open to decision makers for children in care, or on the cusp of care. It provides a framework which assists care planning and helps to monitor and evaluate policies and practices. The matrix shows placement options along the horizontal axis and levels of legal interventions going up the vertical axis. Imaginative use of the various combinations provide possibilities to ensure that children are well placed and safe; that parents are appropriately and adequately supported and that resources are deployed to maximum effect:

Decision-making matrix for looked after children

Interim care order (ICO) or care order (CO)	Placement with parents, etc. Regulations	Approved as kinship foster carers	Care plan to assess type and goals of placement, family contact etc.
	7	**8**	**9**
Legal action, but not ICO or CO	Care proceedings but no order, or interim supervision order/ supervision order, possible use of emergency protection order (EPO) or police powers of protection (PPP) at start	Care proceedings but no order, or ICO/CO, possible use of EPO/PPP at start	Care proceedings but no order, possible use of EPO/PPP at start
	4	**5**	**6**
No legal action	s.17 Family Support	Possible support via s. 17 money; possibly s. 20	s. 20 accommodation
	1	**2**	**3**
	Placed with parents or people with PR	**Placed with extended family or friends**	**Placed in foster care or residential care**

(Dickens, Howell, Thorburn and Schofield (2007))

As the authors point out, supporting children in their own home is the preferred option and the most cost-effective. All of the options, from 1 to 8 can be employed to reduce the numbers of children getting into box 9 which is a formal care setting, and the most expensive option. Finally, Dickens *et al.* (2007) conclude that the challenge is not simply to reduce the numbers of children in care, but to strike a balance between the safety and well-being of children, support to families and to maximise limited resources. In particular, it is to ensure that resources are deployed efficiently and effectively to keep children at home and to return home when possible and only those children who really need to be in care are separated from their families and wider community.

Protecting children in care

Ambivalence and assumptions

There is a long and disturbing history of state indifference towards the plight of children in its care. For centuries these children represented an underclass that did not, and were not allowed to intrude upon the daily lives of mainstream society. Such children were better kept out of sight and out of mind. Corby *et al.* (2001) argue that residential care was used as a punitive measure to deter families from breaking up and as a means of controlling young offenders and that the neglect and abuse of such children in care has not been a major consideration in history. Violations within institutions often go unnoticed or without comment, with only the most salacious incidents of exploitation making for eye-catching headlines (Davies, 2005). Revelations of institutional abuse in Jersey in 2008 is a case in point. Wolmar (2000) argues that if, instead of 'sexual abuse', terms such as rape and buggery were used, more people might have taken notice.

In order to fully understand the reasons why children have been harmed in state care, it is necessary to examine a complex range of factors that are rooted in the historical development of state sponsored institutions, and the cultural practices that lead children to be viewed as 'non-citizens' and 'a problem' (Bessant and Hil, 2005). The ambivalence shown towards such children has led to a sustained lack of concern regarding the maintenance of standards. One contemporary indicator of this indifference is the low qualification levels of staff working in children's homes (Crimmens, 2000).

In Ireland, following extensive political debate on the issue of institutional abuse, legislation was passed in 2002 which established the Residential Institutions Abuse Redress Board (RIRB) to make awards to persons who were abused in the care of institutions. The scale of abuse in institutions is reflected in the scale of payments made to the victims. To date over three thousand payments have been made (RIRB, 2008).

The Utting report (1997) did much to highlight concerns regarding children living away from home and to improve safeguards for such children. Its very title, *People Like Us*, is a comment on the need for a societal shift in values towards such children. The report *Modernising Social Services* (DoH, 1998) followed soon after. It accepted that too many reports and inquiries have highlighted that children in the care of the state were neglected and abused and it urged local authorities not to lose focus on the most vulnerable children. The second Joint Chief Inspectors report (2005) commented that: 'There is still an assumption that because these children are . . . in care or under supervision, they must be safe . . .' Finally the report *Care Matters* (DfES, 2006) pledged that care should make a positive difference in children's lives. However, although there has been a positive shift in societal values towards children in care, the ability of social services to keep children safe in care cannot be taken for granted.

Making children's safety an explicit objective

The second Joint Chief Inspectors report (2005) identified a number of key areas for improvement, including:

- Contact for all children with people to whom they can express their views or concerns.
- Practices in relation to the physical control of children in many settings where children are cared for.
- Ensuring that there are policies and procedures for protection in all settings.
- Priority to safeguard the needs of all children.
- Consistent monitoring arrangements.
- Effective recruitment and staff checking systems.

Together these key areas combine to provide a safer environment for children, but only if they are acted upon. Clearly managers have a key part to play in ensuring that this happens. They are in a position to influence organisational culture by, for example, equating working with children in care as being of equal value and importance to protecting children in the community.

Much is made lately of outcomes for children in care. We know, for example, that educational attainment and health status tend to be diminished for children in the care system due, in some measure, to the priorities afforded them by professionals (Parker *et al.*, 1991; Winter, 2006). In the same way as we wish to make improvements in these areas, it would be a modest but important outcome intention that each child might have a safe journey through care. Instead of taking child protection as a given, questions should be asked under each of the bullet points above as to what actions managers might take to improve services to children in the critical areas identified above.

Managing the care system

The role of senior management

The overall governance of the care system cannot be left to others while senior managers get on with 'more important things'. The Social Service Inspectorate report, *Building a Better Future for Children* (2004) states: 'good leadership is demonstrated when children are the focus at the top of the organisation . . .' This is wise counsel. In a similar vein, the Department for Education and Skills report, *Care Matters* (2006) advises that 'every councillor, every Director of Children's Services, every social worker or teacher should demand no less for each child in care than they would for their own children'. Corporate parenting needs to be owned at the top if it is to be a reality across the organisation.

Political, social and economic factors have created a demand for greater transparency and accountability across public services. Social work, which had a strong tradition of individualism, has had to make a major adjustment where professional practice is now measured against pre-determined standards. The powers and duties of social services are now more prescriptive, thereby reducing the scope of individual professional discretion (Munro, 2004). Much of the regulation and audit that has crept into mainstream practice of late has much to do with managing risk by making people more accountable. Indeed it has been argued (Culpitt, 1999) that new public management and neo-liberal forms of governance have placed the lessening of risk, not the meeting of need, at the centre of social policy.

Tilbury (2007) questions whether such 'upwards' accountability is effective in improving quality and outcomes and argues that there should also be 'outwards' accountability to the service users. Citing Ashworth *et al.* (2002) Tilbury (2007) lists a set of common problems associated with regulatory regimes:

- Resistance from those regulated by undermining the process in an attempt to retain autonomy.
- Ritualistic compliance, where 'ticking the boxes' may disguise underlying problems of policy or administration.
- Regulatory capture where regulators are unwilling or unable to take action if standards are not met.
- Performance ambiguity when 'good' standards cannot be clearly established.
- Data problems when performance standards are clear but insufficient data makes it difficult to measure compliance.

Decisions regarding the admission of children to care are of such critical importance to their lives that they should not, and cannot, be delegated to frontline staff and junior levels of management alone. More senior management has an obligation to have strategies in place to discharge their legal obligations by addressing alternatives to care, the governance of decision-making regarding the initiation of legal proceedings and admission to care. *Care Matters* (DfES, 2006) states that 'any decision to bring children into care represents such a major step that there should always be senior level involvement in decision-making'.

A management eye should also be cast on the monitoring processes for those children who are in care. Particular attention ought to be paid to the review process to ensure that children who could go home do not get lost in the system. A strategic examination is also required which considers adoption options for children in long term care (HIQA, 2007a) and the careers of all children in care must be managed effectively and efficiently from the day they enter the care system. Whereas these duties can be delegated, they can never be abdicated, and the simple delegation rule of 'hands off, eyes on' always applies.

While much of the public attention has focused on residential care, sight should not be lost of foster care which is where the majority of children are placed. Fostering takes place in a more private domain than residential care; a fact which simultaneously gives rise to monitoring difficulties and opportunities for an abuse of power (Tilbury, 2007). The dispersed nature of foster care placements makes fostered children a much more diverse constituency than those in residential care and, consequently, all the more deserving of particular attention.

Busy and beleaguered frontline staff will often employ various rationing tools as a survival mechanism, but these can have serious and irreparable effects on the children they are employed to serve. Frontline managers can be complicit in such practices by, for example, condoning the fact that some children in care may be left without a social worker or where care plans are not reviewed or, worse, remain unwritten. Often such decisions do not appear on the radar of senior management and, as such, they go unnoticed, unchallenged and unresolved. Given the exhortation in *Care Matters* to do no less for each child in care than one would for one's own children, this represents a case of serious corporate parental neglect.

Whistle-blowing systems must be put in place that alert senior management to the fact that statutory obligations are not being fulfilled. Then decisions can be made regarding the distribution of resources, the re-configuration of services and, if necessary, the alerting of the political system to the inability to meet statutory duties. Ignorance of the fact will be no excuse if such matters are exposed. Over and above the issue of disservice to children there is huge exposure for managers who preside over such practices. When Lord Laming (2003) described 'a gross failure of the system' he pointed the finger at senior management, more so than frontline staff.

Managing strategically

The inability of social services to protect children who were suffering abuse is frequently underpinned by systemic failure as well as practice failure (Calder, 2007). The risk of systemic failure inevitably increases when there is significant or sustained organisational change. Communication pathways become disrupted and knowledge is often dissipated (Johnson and Petrie, 2005). People get displaced and their expertise goes with them. In such conditions strategic management becomes all the more important as a means of controlling the future.

In the context of children in care, strategic management concerns the orchestration of all available placement resources, blending them into a continuum of care that meets the needs of children. It is the art of selecting future courses of action that direct resources to the highest priority or changing needs (Harrison, 2006). Senior management should verify that arrangements for managing care services, within an overall strategy for children's services, are effective (Utting, 1991). Strategic plans should then set out specific aims backed by clear accountability and effective monitoring (SSI, 2004).

In residential care, the physical isolation of children's homes from the management structure of its parent body can set it apart (Utting, 1991). In a study which included a series of interviews with residential managers, Berridge and Brodie (1998) found that from the managers' perspective, profound changes in their services, organisational structures and professional and managerial isolation of children's homes were key issues for them. The study highlighted that in many recent crises in residential care, deficiencies in external management were identified as a significant contributory factor. When services become isolated they also become separated from mainstream accountability and supervisory arrangements. In such circumstances there is a real risk that such services become a law unto themselves, which is a recipe for dangerous practice. This reinforces the importance of overall governance. Children's homes should not behave, or be seen as an island but rather as one element in a continuum of care under a single line management system. The objectives of an individual unit must contribute to the overall corporate aims of the service as a whole (Frost and Harris, 1996).

A strategic approach should also be adopted in relation to fostering services. The Irish Social Services Inspectorate issued a report in relation to the placement of children under twelve years in residential care. They criticised 'the lack of strategic planning in terms of recruiting, supporting and sustaining sufficient care placements to meet identified needs of children of this age who are in care' (HIQA, 2007b). This needs to be undertaken by managers at a sufficiently high level to have an overview of the whole service. The SSI report also stressed the need to develop standardised management practices to facilitate the monitoring of placement decisions. Even if monitoring arrangements are in place at an operational level, senior management needs to have a quality assurance system that can randomly sample individual cases. Unless placements are adequately monitored and adequately supported they are not likely to provide a quality care experience for children (Cuddenback, 2004).

Main Messages
- Even a positive care experience is an adversity in the life of a child and should therefore be avoided if at all possible.
- If more were done to help parents cope, there would be fewer children in care.
- There is an association between high numbers in care and a lack of strategic planning and under-developed family support services.
- Decisions made at a higher level help to reduce admissions to care.
- The safety of children in care cannot be taken for granted and should be a strategic objective.
- Good leadership is demonstrated when children are the focus of attention at the top of the organisation.
- Unless placements are adequately monitored and supported they are unlikely to provide a quality care experience.

CHAPTER 6

Managing for results

Linking national objectives to local effort

A measure as to whether a national policy is working is its relevance to the workers who knock on doors delivering the service. If it is not affecting the practice of frontline staff, then it is not working. Too often national policies are launched with all due pomp and ceremony only to go disregarded by frontline staff who feel disconnected from the policy intention. This is because it is perceived as something that only happens 'up there'. It is reflective of social exclusion, similar to how a poor family might cast a jaundiced eye on the Government's latest anti-poverty initiative. Therefore, putting policy into practice does not happen spontaneously: it requires leadership.

A challenge for those in leadership positions is to foster a culture that is open to new and creative ways of doing things differently in order to improve outcomes. Very often in social care, staff resist change by use of the 'R word' (resources). A common perception is that doing things differently takes more time and money, but this is not necessarily so. Sometimes it is more about a shift in attitude than a shift of resources. For example, as discussed in Chapter 3, change might be achieved by putting families at the centre of decision-making through the extended use of family group conferencing, or by genuinely taking into consideration the voice of the child when decisions are made.

The current national policies for children are in themselves incontestable as aspirations: like motherhood and apple pie they are difficult to oppose. The five outcomes in *Every Child Matters* (2003) are an example:

1. be healthy
2. stay safe
3. enjoy and achieve
4. make a positive contribution
5. achieve economic well-being

So too are the seven outcomes cited in Agenda for Children's Services (OMC, 2007). It synthesises various types of outcomes found in contemporary children's policy into one single list that it refers to as the Seven National Outcomes for Children in Ireland:

- health, both physically and mentally
- supported in active learning
- safe from accidental and intentional harm
- economically secure
- secure in the immediate and wider physical environment

- part of positive networks of family, friends, neighbours and community
- included and participating in society

Every Child Matters (2003) recognises the need for leadership to do things differently than before. It states that the *Children Act 2004* gives a particular role to local authorities to secure the co-operation of partner organisations, as integration is a cornerstone of the policy. However, the Ofsted report (2008) which followed the Baby P tragedy in Haringey, found that social care, health and police authorities did not adequately communicate or collaborate. It also found that there was insufficient strategic leadership and management oversight of the process of safeguarding children and young people. Consequently, the Department of Children, Schools and Families and the Department of Health is to establish a taskforce aimed at strengthening leadership and management capacity. New Zealand goes so far as to make leadership in children's services a strategic priority. *Leading for Outcomes* (Child, Youth and Family, 2007) states that leadership asks more of us, but that it is now time to step forward on issues that affect children and families and 'to believe in the ability of ourselves and those we work with to create positive change'.

In the face of practice reforms, directors of children's' services may be faced with the challenge of distributing their resources over a wide range of activities in order to move closer to the new policy requirements. In meeting these requirements, directors have to consider:

- How resources are distributed.
- Why they are distributed in that way.
- What evidence is there of the effectiveness of different services.
- How to interpret the evidence.
- What changes they are in a position to make.

(Beecham and Sinclair, 2007)

It is not always appropriate to do everything with a 'big bang'. Sometimes incremental change is both appropriate and prudent. This approach is reflected in Northern Ireland's ten year strategy for children and young people. *Our Children and Young People – Our Pledge* (2006) pledges to promote a move towards prevention and early intervention, but without taking attention away from the children and young people most in need of targeted attention. This is a very realistic approach to strategic planning.

The essence of contemporary children's policy is that every child should be enabled to fulfil their potential. However, according to Beecham and Sinclair (2007), this new vision encompasses five quite different types of strategies:

1. Broad national initiatives aimed at tackling poverty and other sources of deprivation.
2. Initiatives aimed at deprived communities with the intention of improving the lives of children within them.
3. Services intended for families at an early stage of difficulty.
4. Specialist services aimed at resolving specific problems affecting children.
5. Services for children for whom the state has assumed responsibility, or for whom this is a real possibility.

The life expectancy of most policy initiatives, according to Glass (2001) is 'brutish and short'. He argues that as part of the political process, perception, or how a policy is viewed is as important as what it actually does. As such, it is subject to the slings and arrows of political fortune and likely to change as perceptions alter. In essence any reform aimed at providing better outcomes for children and families is carried out on three levels: at the political level where national policy is devised; senior management level where policy is linked to practice; and at practitioner level where the changes have to be delivered. Essentially it is about integrating policy, procedural guidance and core practice into one set that is evidence-based, up to date and accessible (Child, Youth and Family, 2007).

In this regard the Office of the Minister for Children has done a creditable job in combining the three levels of policy making, senior management and practice into one policy framework. *Agenda for Children's Services* (DoH&C, 2007) is a broad policy framework that aims to assist policy makers, managers and frontline practitioners to engage in reflective practice and effective delivery, informed by Irish and international best practice. The document is accompanied by three booklets: one for policy makers, one for senior managers and one for service managers and practitioners that poses a number of reflective questions for each. The policy document itself identifies five service characteristics needed to achieve good outcomes:
1. Connecting services with family and community strengths.
2. Ensuring quality services.
3. Opening access to services.
4. Delivering integrated services.
5. Planning monitoring and evaluating.

The reflective questions in the accompanying booklet concern each of these headings. This is a very inclusive approach that brings policy makers, managers and practitioners together into a cohesive force that is needs-led, evidence-based and outcomes-focused. It provides a clear methodology for linking national objectives to local effort.

The 'what works' agenda

One might well ask how child protection work contributes to the fulfilment of the overall national objectives for children. By and large this work is carried out in the shadows of society, out of the lime light and at a micro-level, where mainstream society does not have to witness it. Clearly child protection work contributes to keeping children safe, but it is often confined to this corner of the national objectives and as such would benefit by being more aligned with the more positive aspirations that society wants for its children.

'What works?' can only be decided in terms of agreed objectives and this raises a question, 'Agreed by whom?' There is a certain ambiguity over the extent to which 'what works' for families, 'what works' for children and 'what works' for society as a whole. It may well be more pragmatic to ask 'what is worth doing for children?' rather than 'what works?' (Glass, 2001). Each of these tiers has a different perspective than the other and, as discussed in relation to putting policy into practice, there needs to be a synergy between the three views of the world before desired outcomes can be agreed.

Even when working at a micro-level where children and families are the focus of attention, it is possible to take into account the multiple influences in a child's social network beyond their immediate parents. Typically there are two types of interventions: small scale responses that are targeted on particular difficulties or a broad approach that tackles social issues. However, it is possible to combine both approaches (Hill, 1995). Key characteristics of a successful project have been identified as intensive work with children and families in the context of a comprehensive approach, which also seeks to change resource distribution and policies to meet the need of vulnerable people (Rosenbeg and Holden, 1992).

The typical approach of social care organisations is to apply casework as a cure-all for most ills. However, there is a growing realisation, particularly in the USA, that more targeted interventions are more likely to have the desired effect on particular problems (Harrison, 2006). Traditionally programmes were designed in response to emotional appeals, for example homeless children, rather than a clear analysis of data and a good understanding of the nature of the problem (Ketter, Moroney and Martin, 1999). In this regard it is important for managers not to be 'led up the garden path' by the political flavour of the month, otherwise resources may well end up being re-directed at the wrong cause.

Critical preconditions for a human service model of management have been identified as:

1. Clearly articulated and achievable goals based on valid data.
2. Enforcement of worker accountability for achieving results.
3. Facilitation of staff behaviour and implementation of activities that bring results.
4. Objective methods of evaluation.
5. Securing the necessary resources for ongoing activities.
6. Facilitation of personal and professional growth.
7. Simplification of bureaucratic procedures.
8. Development of ongoing problem solving and change mechanisms.
9. Goal orientated case management as a basic strategy.
10. Creation of ongoing mechanisms for effecting sound inter-organisational relations.

(Sarri and Hasenfeld, 1978)

There is an emerging recognition of the importance of systematic interventions and on the need to consider the wider environmental influences and policies in relation to family-based interventions. A systems framework recognises the place of strategies targeted at preventing stresses and difficulties from occurring, or having a significant effect, as well as interventions aimed at reducing or removing such strains or difficulties (Hill, 1995). Typically the approach to welfare work with children was to look no further than the family circumstances, often failing to address the way in which children's development is also influenced by the wider community context in which such development is taking place (Gill and Owen, 2007). However, current national policy provides an opportunity to take a more multi-dimensional approach to problem solving. For example, some of the reflective questions for service managers and practitioners in *Agenda for Children's Services* (2007) are:

- Do I fully consider the potential, along with the limitations, of families' informal social networks in making assessments and planning interventions?
- Am I delivering services in a way that complements the informal supports that families have?

The development and use of ecological practice with children and families in disadvantaged communities is explored further in Chapter 7.

Outcomes

Accountability for success lies fairly and squarely at the door of managers. The new approach to managing social services is less about administration and more about requiring managers to be more decisive in determining policy, utilising resources and evaluating outcomes (Harlow and Lawler, 2000). Social work organisations have learned to develop strategic management plans, are more transparent and are getting better at directing services towards the achievement of policy objectives (Adams, 1998). However, as Magura and Silverman Moses (2001) observe, weary of relying on well-intentioned but often less than effective programmes, society is now asking social workers to prove that their work is worth supporting.

There is an assumption that service standards that are monitored will result in better outcomes. However, high standards of compliance do not necessarily mean that children will be better protected or that their well-being has measurably improved (Ministry of Children and Youth Services, 2005). The move towards managing for outcomes represents a move away from the traditional methodology of imposed compliance via inspection and monitoring. The focus on outcomes is less concerned with the process of how things are done and more concerned with the results of what is done.

Parker *et al.* (1995) pose the question, 'Outcomes for whom? They identify five kinds of outcomes in child care:

1. Public outcomes – where public money is expended and public expectation is, or is not, met.
2. Services outcomes – which address the management perspective of overall organisational performance.
3. Professional outcomes – representing staff expectation of what they are trying to achieve.
4. Family outcomes – it is important to consider which outcomes are considered important for the family as a whole.
5. Children's outcomes – consideration of what outcomes are important for the child.

Messages from Research (DoH, 1995) continues to be an insightful and relevant report, expounding, as it does, the need to concentrate on improved outcomes for children. It argues that the events leading up to a referral are usually not as important as the context in which they occur. It advocated that it is better to consider a child to be in need rather than at risk and to go about meeting that need in a way that will provide better outcomes for the family as a whole. This thinking was also in line with contemporary policy in that the outcomes envisage the wider dimensions of the child's life including education, emotional and physical well-being and their position in the family and wider social network.

There is a growing desire to consider what types of interventions are most effective. However, this tendency to assess what works and what does not is linked to the wider political requirement of accountability in the form of performance standards and performance indicators. Inevitably politicians and senior managers are particularly concerned with what represents best value for money (Hill, 1995). Cheetham et al. (1992) were pioneers on the issue of effectiveness as they were one of the first to ask, are programmes always planned with specific goals in mind; whose definition of need is to count; and who is to judge?

When all things are said and done there is still no cast iron method of identifying and measuring outcomes that can be directly attributable to a particular intervention. However, in this regard, Parker et al. (1995) identify two important issues: theoretical frameworks and the relationship between intermediate and final outcomes. A conceptual framework provides an opportunity to identify and, to some extent, control the factors which might influence an outcome. Again, the service provided should be seen as part of a wider network, including education and health. In this way, local practice becomes reflective of what is desired by national policy.

Parker et al. (1995) describe a final outcome as the general objectives desired by society for child care and children's development. Intermediate outcomes, on the other hand, are measures of quality of life, including environmental as well as family factors. According to Hill (1995) there are four types of criteria to assess outcomes at the client level:
1. Are the aims achieved?
2. Is the development or functioning of the child improved?
3. What are the views of the participants?
4. What is the status or living situation of the child subsequently?

Evidence-based practice

With regard to evidence-based practice, the basic tenet is that good practice ought to derive from research evidence concerning the nature, causes and pathways of social problems and the effectiveness of particular responses (Hill, 1995). In reality, however, social care is not as consistent as medicine or nursing when it comes to keeping in touch with emerging research evidence. There is often a hiatus between theory and practice with each being performed in a separate silo with each having insufficient regard to the other. In this regard there is a significant challenge for management to develop a culture that invests in continuous learning. This may well involve a financial investment, as management needs to put its money where its mouth is when it comes to facilitating staff to undertake postgraduate learning and research.

Conversely, it has been argued that evidence-based approaches gain even more salience in organisations, such as social services, where fiscal and resource constraints are forcing human resource rationalisations, ongoing restructuring and ever more accountability through monitoring, quality audits and control mechanisms. At its most extreme there is a view, or an implicit notion, that opinion-based judgement is inferior to evidence-based decision-making, and that extraneous factors such as resource constraints and professional values should not contaminate the evaluative process (Webb, 2001). It is important therefore not to throw the baby out with the bathwater by surpassing professional judgement with purely technocratic methodologies.

The flipside of putting research into practice is putting practice into research. Werner Von Braun, the rocket scientist, is attributed with saying: 'Research is what I'm doing when I don't know what I'm doing.' It perfectly describes the exploratory nature of research. However, pursuing the extra-terrestrial theme, research provides a 'blue skies' version of how things might be. It strives for the gold standard and an ideal reality, and rightly so. However, managing practice takes place in the real world with all its imperfections, where staff go sick or leave and where resources are never sufficient. Therefore, if research takes place in a rarefied atmosphere, it will never amount to more than a pipe-dream. For this reason it behoves practice to set the agenda for research, rather than the other way around. The pertinent question, therefore, is what can research do to enhance practice by providing new methodologies that work in the real world and are of direct benefit to practitioners?

Measuring performance

The search for the silver bullet

'What gets measured gets done' is the saying, attributed to Peters and Waterman (1982) that has by now become a management maxim. Although it does not provide a very positive start to the concept of measuring performance, it does serve to highlight a feature of human nature that if something is being measured, people will do it. The problem is, of course, there is no guarantee that what is being measured is what people actually want done. There is no 'silver bullet' when it comes to the quest for the ultimate best measure of performance.

Previously in social services, if we are to call a spade a spade, there has been an element of 'widget counting' whereby no relationship was established between the process of gathering information and the ultimate goal of improvement of the client condition. It was like someone at government level acquiring a rudimentary grasp of performance measurement and imposing dubious new demands onto an unsuspecting delivery system without figuring out the precise objective of the exercise. In such a climate demands were made for the collection of activity data which never seemed to be given back in the form of messages for managers or practitioners. Data collection became an end in itself with the consequence that it simply became an irrelevant burden for operational managers who could not relate to its purpose and, consequently, resented being drawn away from their core business to make such returns.

There is still a lingering concentration on process measuring whereby measures such as quantifiable data and timelines have been used as indicators of performance. For example, new performance indicators in the United Kingdom (HM Government, 2008) concentrate upon matters such as the percentage of initial assessments for children's social care carried out within seven days; the percentage of children becoming subject to a child protection plan and numbers in care. There is a similar emphasis in Ireland whereby initial assessments and child abuse and neglect reports are counted and the number and percentage of children in care by type is calculated (HSE, 2008).

An unintended consequence of such reliance on process measures is that they concentrate exclusively on efficiencies such as the ability, or inability, of a service to perform. As such, an inability to meet targets can be used as a bargaining chip to barter for more resources. In a scenario such as this, 'worse becomes good' whereby service providers use waiting lists, higher numbers of child abuse referrals, missed timelines and more children in care as indicators of their inability to cope with demand. This is the antithesis of what is desirable in terms of performance measurement as it sheds no light whatsoever upon client condition as it focuses exclusively on the condition of the service provider.

The motivation to measure performance stems from policy makers who wish to monitor policy implementation; social workers who want to gauge their own effectiveness; managers who wish to consider the broader impact of services and their value; the general public who want good quality combined with cost effectiveness; and users who want choice, appropriate and quality services (Carter et al., 1992). Yet the task of devising client-focused measures is not without its challenges. Many social service organisations endeavour to identify and set objectives and to devise ways of measuring progress towards them. However, the precise measurement of children's well-being and the appropriateness of a child's care have faced formidable technical and conceptual obstacles (Magura and Silverman Moses, 2001). The difficulty is that performance measurement does not always capture what services are actually trying to do (Glass, 2001). It is, therefore, essential that managers of child protection services define and evaluate family and system outcomes in order to meet agency goals and to be accountable to the public.

The focus of child protection agencies should be on results, performance and outcomes as they relate to child safety, child and family well-being and permanency. Managers should seek outcomes that are both performance-based and measurable, such as:

- Identify outcomes and indicators that reflect the mission and goals of the agency.
- Identify both short-term and long-term outcomes and indicators.
- Identify outcomes that are desirable for the child and the family as well as for the system.

- Limit the focus to those outcomes that are most important to the agency's mission and goals.
- Define the indicators and measurements it will use for determining outcomes.
- Identify and implement the programmes, processes and operations that will help the agency to meet the desired outcomes.

(CWLA, 1999)

Why measure performance?

Accountability is probably the most cited reason for measuring performance. It is one of an array of managerial changes that have taken place over the last couple of decades in the ongoing pursuit of improved efficiency, effectiveness and holding services to account. Borrowing from market-based practices, performance measurement represents a shift from old-fashioned public administration, with its focus on budget allocation (input) to a focus on outcomes (outputs). Essentially it is a tool for controlling and managing resources, prompted by public concern regarding public expenditure, managerial competence, accountability and transparency (Carter et al., 1992; Tilbury, 2004).

Scott et al. (2005) identify three areas that are required to promote outcome based accountability. They are an organisational culture that supports learning, adequate managerial skills to analyse data and an information system which is capable of enhancing our understanding of what is happening to individuals and groups of children. Much has been written on the need for robust information systems and rightly so. However, suffice it to say here that whether a manager possesses the latest sophisticated software or a tin box, it needs to be capable of providing information at a family and a systems level. Without sufficient information that is easy to access and analyse, the service will struggle to meet its mission and goals (CWLA, 1999). Data on its own is inert: it requires someone to interpret it before it becomes useful.

Behn (2003) has developed eight purposes that public managers have for measuring performance, which provide a useful synopsis of the issues:

Eight purposes that public managers have for measuring performance

---

The purpose: The public manager's question that the performance measure can help answer:

1. **Evaluate:** How well is my agency performing?
2. **Control:** How can I ensure that my subordinates are doing the right thing?
3. **Budget:** On what programmes, people or projects should my agency spend the public's money?
4. **Motivate:** How can I motivate line staff, middle managers, non-profit and for-profit collaborators, stakeholders and citizens to do the things necessary to improve performance?
5. **Promote:** How can I convince political superiors, journalists and citizens that my agency is doing a good job?

6. **Celebrate:** What accomplishments are worthy of the important organisational ritual of celebrating success?
7. **Learn:** Why is what working or not working?
8. **Improve:** What exactly should who do differently to improve performance?

(Robert D. Behn, Harvard University)

Developing suitable performance indicators

Performance indicators are not neutral entities. The way in which indicators are established can influence the very way in which child abuse and neglect are defined, how resources are allocated, what services are funded, and how outcomes for children are responded to (Tilbury, 2004; Martin and Kettner, 1997). To be of actual benefit, and to avoid well documented risks, performance indicators must be designed and used with care. The right things must be measured in the right way if they are to facilitate management decisions to improve service performance. Conversely, if the wrong things get measured in the wrong way, then the wrong things may well get done (De la Harpe *et al.*, 2008).

While there has been a shift away from negative indicators towards the more positive concept of well-being, it needs to be recognised that the concept of well-being is a social construct that is liable to alter over time in response to societal and cultural changes (Fattore, Mason and Watson, 2007). There are inherent dangers in developing indicators that need to be recognised and dealt with. These include the difficulty in balancing the desire to be fully knowledgeable on the one hand and having a manageable set of indicators on the other; or getting bogged down in the measures themselves instead of focusing on what the indicators are supposed to be measuring (CAWT, 2008).

There is currently a positive move away from process measurement to outcome measurement. Such measures have the advantage of encompassing many processes: for example, they may capture how a process is executed as well as its frequency. It is important that the indicators chosen are relevant both to those who manage the service and those who provide that data. It should also be comparable between place (organisation or part thereof) and time if they are to inform management decision making. This requires data standards as well as the flexibility to factor in contextual influences (De la Harpe *et al.*, 2008). For example, the duration of an assessment might reflect the complexity of a case as much as it denotes efficiency by meeting timelines.

Managing strategically

Making data work for you

Information can be gleaned from a host of sources to enhance the decision-making prowess of managers. Data from individual cases, as well as more formal data sets and up to date demographic data, can combine to provide managers with good quality management information to help plan services, deliver appropriate services, improve quality and review staff performance. Management information systems, when properly maintained, will assist managers to identify recurring issues and unmet needs and to identify service delivery trends (CWLA, 1999). In this regard, managers need to combine information from individual sources, such as case files, and to aggregate such data in order to provide a more strategic view of overall service needs and to prioritise service responses.

By way of example, a survey undertaken in Dublin (Harrison, 2003) entailed a statistical analysis of child abuse and neglect reports and admissions to care over a three year period. Neglect, not surprisingly, was the largest reason for the admission of children to care. In fact, neglect and parental inability to cope/parental illness accounted for sixty-five per cent of all admissions during the period under consideration. The study also revealed that forty-seven per cent of children in care were aged between six and twelve years and that forty-nine per cent of children in care came from families headed by lone parents. Hence, when the data was aggregated in this way it provided a clear message that families, where there are children aged between six and twelve years, headed by a lone parent, and where there is evidence of neglect, parental inability to cope or parental illness, are particularly vulnerable and warrant particular attention. It is important that managers use local information to develop particular strategic responses to localised need, rather than spending all their time feeding the monster that is the national data requirement.

Facilitating front line managers to manage

Each organisation will have, or should have, a strategic plan that encapsulates that organisation's mission, vision, goals and strategies and which sets out the main service priorities for the next few years. The strategic plan focuses the organisation's actions and resources on the priority areas necessary to moving the organisation towards the accomplishment of its goals (CWLA, 1996).The strategic plan in its entirety (the big picture) is the business of senior management, however, local managers will share responsibility for one or more development objectives. In this regard the bigger plan can be scaled down to local and individual levels (Booker, 2008). The sum of any organisation is greater than its parts and a service will not perform properly if people are not willing or able to do their job (Johnson and Williams, 2007). It is vital, therefore, that front line managers are signed up to the overall mission of the organisation and can convey this to their staff in a meaningful manner. This requires leadership, guidance and support from senior management. Local managers need to develop a localised mission statement that is consistent with the national or organisational mission.

In this regard the frontline manager is placed at a point in the organisation that is vital to the effective running of the service. They are the conduit through which information is transmitted from senior management to the front line and from the front line back, so that senior management have a proper sense of what is happening on the ground. In fulfilling this role, frontline managers are what Scragg (2005) describes as the 'hinge' between senior management and front line staff.

By their nature social service teams do not always have an explicit plan. Particularly in the pressurised environment of child protection there is a tendency to operate in 'fire-fighting' mode whereby they deal with issues episodically, starting with the cases that are in flames on any given day. Therefore, front line managers need to be encouraged, and given the space to develop a plan for their part of the service which is reflective of the overall mission of the organisation, while at the same time addressing short term and medium term goals for their particular teams (Harrison, 2006).

In this way, the overall organisation is able to translate its strategic plan into an annual operational plan that integrates long range direction into the daily activities of its constituent parts (CWLA, 1996). The individual elements of a service plan are like stepping-stones to a successful outcome. The localised service plan can provide an overview of services to be provided within a particular timeframe and within existing financial constraints. In addition to encompassing the overall agency mission it also provides key priorities for the various sections of the organisation for the coming year, along with objectives and targets and arrangements for monitoring progress (Harrison, 2006).

Main Messages

- Accountability for success lies fairly and squarely at the door of managers.
- A measure as to whether a national policy is working is its relevance to workers on the ground.
- Sometimes it is a shift in attitude, more than resources, that is required.
- Make leadership a strategic priority.
- Integrate policy, procedural guidance and core practice into one set that is evidence-based.
- Do not surpass professional judgement with technocratic methodologies.
- Data on its own is inert: it requires someone to interpret it before it becomes useful.
- Be less concerned with the process of how things are done and more concerned with the results of what is done.

CHAPTER 7

Managing partnerships with families and communities

The concept of working in partnership has become an important and recognised feature in the delivery of a wide range of policies and services. It has become, in theory at least, the preferred way of addressing complex problems that are not amenable to resolution by any one agency working on its own (Percy-Smith, 2006). Much has been written on the policy and practice aspects of inter-agency and inter-disciplinary co-ordination, co-operation and collaboration. However, the same attention has not been paid to how the same services might engage with children, families and communities and it is, therefore, this aspect of partnership that this chapter addresses.

The meaning of partnership

Attempting to understand what partnership means precisely is not helped by the lack of any clear definition and the huge variation in the types of association to which the term is applied (Harrison *et al.*, 2003). Tennyson (1998) cited by Harrison *et al.* (2003) defines partnership as:

> ... *a cross-sector alliance in which individuals, groups or organisations agree to work together to fulfil an obligation or undertake a specific task; share the risks as well as the benefits; and review the relationship regularly, revising their agreement as necessary.*

Traditionally social services have evolved from a centralist and hierarchal delivery model which did little to promote the ideals of partnership (Cullen, 1998). According to Sullivan and Skelcher (2002) the emerging concept of partnership is a 'new language of public governance' arising from restlessness with conventional state-driven and market-led approaches. Key characteristics of a successful partnership are likely to include:

- Acknowledgement of the existence of a common problem and an agreed vision of what a successful outcome should be.
- An agreed plan of action to address the problem.
- Acknowledgement of, and respect for, the contribution that each can bring to the partnership.
- Accommodation of the different values and cultures of each party in the partnership.
- Information exchange and agreed communication systems.

- Agreed decision-making structures, roles and responsibilities.
- Risk taking.

(Harrison et al., 2003)

The contemporary concept of partnership is usually confined to co-ordination and collaboration between organisations. However, if we are to genuinely engage in a revised worker-service user relationship, expounded in earlier chapters, these key characteristics should equally serve to describe what that revised relationship might look like.

Engaging children and families

A central theme of this book is the requirement for those engaged in welfare and protection work to enter into a more equal relationship with children and families. A leaf might well be taken from the book of the New York City Police Department which developed a strategy encapsulated in the slogan, 'Courtesy, Professionalism and Respect'. The case has long since been made for involving families in decisions that affect them as a means of satisfying natural justice and opening the child protection system up to public scrutiny (Morrison, 1990; Bell, 1999). Willumsen and Skivenes (2005) argue that there must be 'public accessibility' in order to ensure that decision-makers can demonstrate sound reasoning for applying the values and norms that are embedded in the actions they take. For a long time it has been recognised that in managing child protection systems, it is necessary to achieve a balance between a legalistic, protectionist approach and one that offers support and assistance to families (Fox Harding, 1997; Platt, 2001). At this stage it is now axiomatic that there should be a re-focusing of social work practice and the debate has now moved from why this should be so to how it might be achieved (Spratt and Callan, 2004).

However, although social work might perceive itself being 'on the side of the angels' there is an uphill battle to be fought in order for it not to be externally perceived as being in the business of regulation and control (Beresford and Croft, 2004). One of the pioneering studies of user involvement found that, while social workers saw themselves as taking a benevolent approach, the families at the receiving end did not experience benevolence, feeling themselves to be on the wrong end of a heavy-handed, autocratic approach (Corby, 1987). Unfortunately, this experience has been consistently replicated elsewhere in official reports (Cleaver and Freeman, 1995; Farmer and Owen, 1995; Thoburn et al., 1995; Buckley et al., 2008). There is a persistently strong tendency for parents to be highly critical of child protection interventions. Neither can this criticism be seen merely as bias: researchers are agreed that many parents can look beyond their personal experience to offer insightful and sophisticated views on child protection practice as a whole (Dale, 2004).

According to Beresford (2001), social work practitioners have a minimal say in the development of practice and theory and are generally conspicuous by their absence in publications and policy discussions. He argues that re-organisation and managerialism shapes practice and the day-to-day activities of practitioners. Yet, as Spratt (2000, 2001) has demonstrated, social workers tend to revert to child protection type, even when mandated to behave differently. While the re-focusing debate has helped to re-frame child protection work as child welfare work, the concept of risk continues to preoccupy social workers (Spratt and Callan, 2004). Hallett (1995) intimates that social workers welcome the structure and safety afforded by procedures because they help to allay anxiety. Bell (1995) has demonstrated that structures in the agency for managing, supervising and supporting workers in child protection teams are key determinants of their capacity to involve parents. It is, therefore, necessary for managers to provide the leadership that permits staff to work differently (see Chapter 3).

Although it is difficult to reconcile the need to protect children while at the same time affording their parents a sense of integrity, it has to be acknowledged that not all children who come to the attention of child protection services are in danger and less intimidating and more proportionate responses would be both appropriate and beneficial to all concerned (Buckley *et al.* 2008).

Worker-service user relationships

How a service is perceived by a service user is likely to be greatly influenced by the nature of the service being provided. For example, some areas of social work are greatly valued by service users such as specialist hospice and palliative care social work, where practitioners have retained considerable control of their role and are also more visible and influential (Croft *et al.*, 2004).

Yet it is not unreasonable to expect that involuntary recipients of a child protection service will resent the intervention and respond accordingly. To compound matters there is also the fact that many service users have a preconception that child protection social workers are all-powerful, leaving the service user feeling disempowered and stigmatised (Spratt and Callan, 2004; Buckley *et al.*, 2008). However, similar feelings have also been expressed by a very different group of users who voluntarily sought a service. A study on inter-country adoption outcomes found that even applicants who found their assessment a positive experience, still described the process as intrusive and distressing (Greene *et al.*, 2007). This is indicative of a much skewed worker-user relationship.

In the adoption study, what applicants liked the most was when social workers displayed efficiency and professionalism tempered with empathy and respect. Someone who could be described as a 'nice person' rated highly with applicants. This was also observed by Dale (2004) in the context of child protection services, who found that characteristics such as being supportive, being 'matter of fact' and 'being human' were particularly valued by parents. Similarly, a more recent study on the perceptions of service users in the child protection system (Buckley *et al.*, 2008) found that accessibility and reliability were considered to be very important elements of a quality service. Conversely, service users frequently described a lack of respect when their phone calls and messages were not returned and where workers were difficult to find, even at critical moments.

Good manners are a cost-neutral commodity and go a long way to at least having the service user favourably disposed towards the workers. Simple things, such as returning phone calls in a timely manner, matter. It is not always about resources, the system and management; sometimes it is just about staff needing to more consistently display courtesy and respect, even when it may not be reciprocated. It is not easy for workers to hear this, particularly as they perform a fairly thankless job, but it does need to be heard.

There is also an issue here for managers. Those in charge of the service need to foster a culture that places a large importance on the little things that demonstrate respect. It must be recognised by all concerned in the delivery of services that the relationship between the worker and service user is a critical success factor. As alluded to in Chapter 1, Biestek's seminal work on the case work relationship (1961) emphasises the importance of this affiliation and rapport between service provider and service user that provides a powerful bonding agent that stays firm even when the going gets tough.

Complaints mechanisms

Dale (2004), in examining the perspectives of a sample of families on their involvement with child protection services, found that only one of a proportionately high number of dissatisfied families made use of formal complaints structures. He therefore concludes that managers at all levels may not even be aware of the extent of the dissatisfaction. Furthermore, in that study, two families consciously decided not to complain in case they might be even more punitively treated. Similarly, in the study undertaken by Buckley et al. (2008), the lack of publicised information about how to make a complaint was seen by some service users as a deliberate ploy to put them off using it. Worse still, others chose not to use the complaints procedure lest it backfired on them.

It is evident, therefore, in a system where users are inclined to believe that the dice is loaded against them, that managers must be positively proactive in encouraging consumer feedback and complaints by publicising the system in ways that are attractive and welcoming to service users. A hallmark of a quality service is its ability to take criticism on the chin in the interest of raising standards.

Parental involvement and participation

At least until the mid- to late 1990s, there is evidence to suggest that the involvement of service users was perceived by them as being unbeneficial and tokenistic (Campbell, 1996). In 1995 a number of studies emerged in the United Kingdom which dealt with the perspectives and perceptions of families (Cleaver and Freeman, 1995; Farmer and Owen, 1995; Thoburn et al., 1995). The policy and practice of parental involvement began to emerge at this time, affording researchers an opportunity to evaluate practice from the perspective of both the professionals and the caregivers (Buckley et al., 2008). In Ireland, Buckley et al. (1997) showed how parental involvement was still in its infancy in the mid- to late 1990s. At that time the majority of professionals preferred parents to have only partial attendance at case conferences, justifying this by declaring that parents would be overwhelmed or intimidated.

More recently Dale (2004) demonstrated how parents do indeed experience fear and upset while attending child protection conferences. Not that that is a reason for denying them access to the process. In this study, the most common parental concern was the attendance of so many people whom they did not know. Buckley *et al.* (2008) also noted that parents felt overwhelmed, but the discomfort diminished when there were subsequent conferences and parents got to know people better. For parental attendance and participation at conferences to be meaningful, considerable preparation is required. Good intentions alone will not level the playing field between service user and service provider. As there is an asymmetrical balance of power and knowledge between both sides, it is necessary to build in formal structures so that participants are really heard and can take part in a collaborative process that is to their satisfaction (Willumsen and Skivenes, 2005).

Family Welfare Conferencing (or Family Group Conferencing as it is referred to in the UK and elsewhere) which takes a more strengths-based approach to family problem solving and actively engages families in decision-making, appears to be more acceptable to parents (O'Brien, 2000; Bell and Wilson, 2006). However, even then, there is still evidence of professional resistance to this form of power sharing with families (O'Brien, 2000; Brown, 2003). In the study of user's perceptions undertaken by Buckley *et al.* (2008), only three of fifty-four participants attended a family welfare conference but they found it a positive experience. Tantalisingly, the reason for this low uptake is not explained.

There appears to be little co-relationship between parents having a positive experience of the proceedings of a conference and their satisfaction with the outcome. In Dale's study (2004) several parents reported being baffled and offended when, following the trauma of investigation and conferencing, their child was placed on the 'at risk register' but they could then fall into a 'black hole' with no subsequent contact from the social services. Buckley *et al.* (2008) also found that parents' dissatisfaction was augmented when they felt no positive change had occurred in the family's situation following the case conference. While one cannot expect that parents will always agree with the outcome of a conference, there is an onus on professionals to ensure that they are at least crystal clear about what that outcome is and that they are kept informed of subsequent developments.

Beresford and Croft (2004) contend that the trend towards user participation needs to be understood in the context of movements of health and social care services users such as disabled people, survivors' movements and mental health service users. These have developed a new discourse which challenges traditional social work and takes a rights-based approach to service consumption. Beresford and Croft (2004) argue further that what they term 'managerialist related approaches' have led to little or no transfer of power and decision-making. Yet, as has been demonstrated, social workers can be resistant to such change: the relinquishing of power is seldom willingly conceded. There is, therefore, a role for managers in championing the change by promoting the concept of service users as customers and therefore striving for customer satisfaction. This may entail an exercise in quality assurance whereby managers undertake a random sample of cases and elicit the views of service users on the quality of the services. Such proactive measures are justifiable, particularly in the light of Dale's (2004) conclusion that the absence of complaints may mean that managers are actually unaware of the level of user dissatisfaction.

Involving children and young people

While the needs and interests of children are often similar to those of their parents, they must be seen as separate and distinct (Gilligan, 1999). Although much lip service has recently been paid to this concept, it does not always convert into professional practice. A paradox exists whereby there is considerable talk within social work about listening to children while, at the same time, often failing to do just that. Young people often complain that social workers do not listen (Morgan, 2005: 2006). The power that is invested in professionals by legislation and agency function may lead them to believe that they are expected to know best, and this belief will shape their interventions and transactions with children. Furthermore, when it does involve children, mainstream social work tends to fit them into decision-making models that were designed for adults (Nixon, 2007).

The mandate for the meaningful involvement of children and young people is clearly asserted in the *UN Convention on the Rights of the Child* (UNCRC):

Parties shall assure to the child who is capable of informing his or her own views the right to express those views freely in all matters affecting the child, the views of the child being given due weight in accordance with the age and maturity of the child.

(Article 12.1)

The Irish Government embedded this concept in the *National Children's Strategy* (2000), establishing a national goal that 'Children will have a voice'. Unfortunately, this is not always how children experience their interactions with social workers. For example, in a recent study (Buckley *et al.*, 2008), some young people spoke about social worker interactions where their parents' views were taken on board more than theirs and where they felt that their viewpoints were not considered or were ignored.

According to Sinclair and Franklin (2001) children's participation can be facilitated by:
- the provision of information
- consultation and continuous dialogue
- preparation
- taking account of the child's needs
- treating children with respect
- giving feedback

Managers need to counter any professional resistance to the participation of children and young people by acting as a change agent for their staff, nurturing the necessary culture shift. This may well have resource implications if, for example, training is required to bring about the necessary movement of hearts and minds.

Another reason for managers to encourage the participation of children and young people is the fact that it results in better decision-making (McNeish and Newman, 2001). Children value the experience of being consulted and being listened to (Bell and Wilson, 2006). The ability of professionals to communicate with genuineness and respect is also valued by young people. How young people perceive the child protection system is greatly influenced by whether they viewed the intervention as something they were subject to or in which they were active agents. Again, this further demonstrates the key importance of a quality relationship (Buckley *et al.*, 2008).

Engaging communities

The traditional methods of delivering statutory child welfare and protection services do not naturally lead themselves to engagement with communities. Service providers tend to abide by rigid professional and bureaucratic boundaries that do not lend themselves to multi-disciplinary or inter-agency co-operation (Cullen, 1998). The episodic nature of casework predisposes social workers to look at families as 'cases' in isolation from any community context.

This is compounded by the fact that child abuse is defined in a legalistic manner, reducing and categorising various behaviours into particular types of 'abuse'. To a large extent the 'professionalisation' of child protection tends to locate culpability within individual families which facilitates the notion of them being dealt with as individual 'cases'. However, the fact of the matter is that families do not see themselves as cases; they see themselves as a set of unique individuals with a unique set of difficulties.

Definitions

Families do not think in accordance with formal categories of child protection systems where complex situations are categorised into discrete events such as 'physical abuse', 'sexual abuse', 'emotional abuse' and 'neglect'. For this reason Dale (2004) substituted the traditional classification of 'abuse type' to more accurately reflect the perspective of families. For example, physical abuse was referred to as 'physical injury', thus eliminating the implication of intent.

In England, a piece of research undertaken by the National Society for the Prevention of Cruelty to Children, aimed to gain an understanding of the issues that concerned families in a local community. The findings of this research showed that most parents worried about drug abuse, paedophiles and heavy traffic; while children worried about bullying, unsafe roads and the lack of safe areas in which to play (Wright, 2004). This reinforces the fact that there are a plethora of hazards that are not reflected in official categorisation of child abuse and yet are extremely pertinent to the protection of children. A prerequisite to seeing families in the context of their communities is the need to extend the official language of abuse to include the many injustices that are done to children by society, as well as the few that are done to them by parents.

Mondy and Mondy (2004) describe a project in Australia where child protection programmes are perceived as a valuable source of inspiration for communities. NEWPIN, a centre-based child protection and parent intervention programme, substitutes the suspicious nature of child abuse investigation with a strengths-based approach that provides parents with a safe place that allows them to modify their behaviour and increase their knowledge about child protection issues, using the solidarity of peer support. In NEWPIN there are no 'bad parents'; there are only 'parents who are trying to do the best for their kids' or 'parents who are being the best parent they can be', thereby emphasising the positive aspects of change.

Those who have regular contact with families have a unique opportunity to receive information regarding the interplay between individuals and the social and physical world they occupy, and the ways in which families are supported or undermined by the characteristics of the environments which they inhabit. An ecological perspective can be gained whereby the connections between the different areas of their lives can be understood. For example, parents may identify family tensions that are associated with housing problems, or the behaviour of a child that is linked to what is happening at school (Gill and Jack, 2007).

Associated with this is another issue with which those managing services need to be cognisant. Buckley et al. (2008) demonstrated situations in which requests for help were perceived by service users to have 'backfired'. For example, a case where a service user had drawn attention to parenting difficulties they were experiencing with very young children resulted in their children being removed to care very quickly. Understandably the parent felt that having initiated a request for help, they should have been positively affirmed and alternative, more helpful, responses should have been provided. Interpretation of the facts, and a proportionate response to them, are vitally important and need to be embedded in the very soul of child protection teams by those who lead them. Paradoxically, playing safe may have the same effect of the cure being worse than the disease. Consequently, calculated risk-taking is good.

Working with neighbourhoods

As members of a community, families experience their lives holistically, not merely as a series of distinct compartments. Indeed, in the UK, official guidance (1995) stressed the importance of managers taking responsibility for negotiating good working relationships with others and adopting joint approaches to involvement, participation and partnership with families. Effective relationships between community representatives and service providers are an ideal way of identifying gaps and enabling solutions (Maguire and Truscott, 2006). It can add 'another string to the bow' of service providers whereby such collaboration can enhance their capacity to be effective. Whereas episodic casework is the equivalent of storm troopers parachuting in, a neighbourhood approach is the equivalent of the 'bobby on the beat', sharing resources, exchanging information and picking up vital local knowledge.

According to Davies (2004) the effective safeguarding of children requires a dual strategy of prevention and protection and the community has a vital role to play in both. The community can help to encourage the recognition of abuse allowing for earlier intervention and can also contribute to universal solutions to the causes of child abuse that are associated with social and economic disadvantage. Davies (2004) also provides a reminder that child abuse is not solely located within families; there is also a global child abuse industry that needs to be countered by protective community strategies. In the Victoria Climbié inquiry report, Lord Laming (2003) commented that the eyes and ears of the community were not used enough to identify children who were in need.

If a community network is in place to inform the professional response through involvement in appropriate referral and participation in intervention strategies, children will have enhanced protection from all forms of abuse, not just that which is located within families (Davies, 2004). Such a community development approach engages communities in promoting children's welfare and extends responsibility for their safety and well-being beyond the domain of health and social services (Bell, 2004). There are obvious advantages for professionals in harvesting the resources of communities. They can provide a valuable early warning system and a direct source of referral to specialist services when they are required (Cullen, 1998).

According to Coulton et al. (2007) there are two major traditions that influence the thinking about the relationships between neighbourhoods and child maltreatment. The first concerns the relationship between geographic concentrations of social problems within neighbourhoods. Citing Testa and Furstenberg (2002) they point out that, as far back as the 1900s, social workers and sociologists had made the connection with the tendency for delinquent and neglected children to concentrate geographically. The second tradition, led by developmental psychology, concerns how child development and parenting is influenced by the environment, including the neighbourhood.

Both of these traditions are relevant to the management of child welfare and protection services for they bring their own insights to the causation of maltreatment while, at the same time, prompting solutions focused on neighbourhoods rather than individual families. The United States Advisory Board on Child Abuse and Neglect (1993) coined the phrase 'prevention zones' to describe geographically targeted neighbourhoods to reduce child maltreatment. From a management perspective it is a good use of resources to target communities that share endemic problems rather than dealing with events within individual families on an episodic basis.

Nelson and Baldwin (2004) describe an exercise in comprehensive neighbourhood mapping to improve children's safety from sexual crime. It involves imaginatively gathering and interpreting information concerning young people's safety within a defined geographical area which, in turn, involves agencies and communities working together to identify problems and seek solutions to them. The exercise revealed considerable socio-economic and health disadvantage. It prompted a need to target particular groups of carers for support in keeping their children safe. For example, the audit showed that fifty-seven per cent of the women in the neighbourhood had their first child between the age of sixteen and nineteen years of age. Nelson and Baldwin (2004) also make the valid observation that current protection systems that react to individual cases do not factor in the differences between communities.

Similarly, statistical information can be used to direct services towards constituencies or communities where particular forms of disadvantage are prevalent. For example, in one Irish Health Board area, in a statistical analysis of child abuse reports and children in care (Harrison, 2003), different information sources combined to provide powerful indications as to which children were most vulnerable in the community. Most children in the care system were aged between six and twelve years. Child abuse, other than neglect was not a significant reason for admission to care. The two most common reasons for admission, accounting for sixty-five per cent, were neglect, and parental inability to cope. In addition, half of the children in care came from families headed by lone parents. Inevitably, most of these lone parents were women, for it is indeed a true maxim that when the going gets tough, the men get going. From this analysis it was apparent that the children most at risk in the community were those aged between six and twelve years, particularly those with single parents where there was evidence of neglect or parental inability to cope. Scarce resources could therefore be targeted at communities where conditions featured prominently.

Moving from a casework system to a more community development style approach probably ticks all the boxes in terms of contemporary national policies and in terms of an approach to partnership at local level. However, without major adjustments to working practices and professional culture within mainstream children's services, it will not become a reality. What is required is an understanding of the importance of working in partnership with disadvantaged neighbourhoods, gathering and analysing information about the community's circumstances and by developing local indices of child well-being as a means of complementing ongoing efforts to monitor high risk individuals and families (Jack, 2006). Once again, it must be said that such a fundamental shift in practice will not necessarily be embraced by social workers whose training and practice to date has been steeped in the casework tradition. It will take vigorous leadership by managers to change unhelpful attitudes (DoH, 1995).

Main Messages

- Partnership is an ideal way of addressing complex problems that are not amenable to resolution by any one agency working on its own.
- Involving families in decision-making satisfies natural justice and opens the child protection system up to public scrutiny.
- Not all children who come to the attention of child protection services are in danger and more proportionate responses might be appropriate.
- A human touch, accessibility and reliability matters to families.
- Managers must proactively encourage consumer feedback and complaints.
- Effective safeguarding of children requires a dual strategy of prevention and protection and the community has a vital role to play in both.

CHAPTER 8

Managing staff welfare and protection

Staff welfare is a management issue

Staff welfare is a management issue; or at least it should be. In purely mercenary terms, a contented workforce is good for productivity and overall effectiveness and negates the costs associated with staff replacement, such as recruitment and induction not to mention the loss of knowledge that is incurred with the departure of every staff member. Managers are well advised to focus attention on factors that are known to promote job satisfaction among staff, such as opportunities for personal growth and chances to develop their repertoire of professional skills on the job. Browne (2000) cites Locke's Value Theory (Locke, 1976) which asserts that the more people receive outcomes they value the more satisfied they will be, and the less they receive such outcomes the more dissatisfied they will be. Therefore, an effective way to satisfy staff is to find out what they want and, to the extent possible, give it to them (Browne, 2000).

Two major assumptions are often made with regard to the issue of staff contentment and retention. The first is that departing employees will give managers full and accurate reasons for leaving and secondly, that it is possible to identify a single, most salient reason for leaving. In reality, however, employees often have good reason to withhold the whole truth and are often economical with it. Often the real reasons are mixed up, but might be summed up as either pull or push factors. Pull factors represent a positive attraction to alternative employment, while push factors are likely to be associated with organisational culture, disapproval of change or perceptions of unfairness (Taylor, 2002).

A number of cultural assumptions run deep in management practice. Anglo-Saxon culture tends to hold a universalistic view of the world, whereby the rules and obligations to a wider society are a strong source of moral reference. Individualistic cultures that prevail in Britain and Ireland choose the individual and pay the price of impaired teamwork and the tendency to push for personal objectives even when they damage the team as a whole. Conversely, collective cultures, prevalent for example in Japan, tend to choose the group over the individual (Browne, 2000).

In a time of increased globalisation, managers have started to cotton onto the cultural requirements of ethnic client groups. However, much less management attention has been paid to the cultural norms of staff who, increasingly, hail from many different places and backgrounds. The diverse backgrounds of service users and service providers alike have come to characterise life on the ground in many metropolitan areas (Parton, 2004) and, as such, provide managers real opportunities to avail of fresh thinking and to try new approaches to decision-making that are not embedded in an Anglo-Saxon comfort-zone.

Staff satisfaction and dissatisfaction

As a general rule there are four key elements that will positively contribute to the promotion of job satisfaction in any employment setting (Browne, 2000):

1. **Pay people fairly:** this can be a bone of contention within social care where those nearest to the services user tend to be paid the least. However it can be compensated for by extrinsic rewards such as opportunities for promotion or professional growth.
2. **Improve the quality of supervision:** satisfaction is high when supervisors are considered competent.
3. **Decentralise the control of organisational power:** it is best when the capacity to make decisions is invested in several people, not just one, or a few. Job satisfaction is enhanced when staff believe that they have some impact on their organisation.
4. **Match people to jobs:** when the job is congruent with their interests staff satisfaction follows.

Conversely, in the context of child welfare and protection work, reasons for dissatisfaction and factors influencing decisions to leave, have been cited by Westbrook *et al.* (2006) as the psychological and physical stress associated with the work; changes for the worst (such as increased bureaucracy); nostalgia for the way things used to be; and a belief that working in child care has become much more complex with societal change, reflected in increased risk of violence, drugs, HIV and other ills in which many vulnerable families are embedded.

Specific issues relating to working conditions in child welfare and protection agencies present many challenges which lead to a very stressful working environment. (Westbrook *et al.*, 2006). These include:

- inadequate compensation
- large caseloads
- long hours
- voluminous paperwork associated with strict policy requirements
- personal safety issues
- inadequate training and supervision
- involuntary clients with complex problems
- lack of adequate resources with which to service clients
- lack of promotional opportunities
- high staff turnover adversely affecting those who remain and
- adverse media and public opinion

Stress

There is no such thing as an optimum level of stress. What some perceive as comfortable will be perceived as crushing by others. In general terms, when stress is present in the workplace it is often associated with excessive productivity goals, convoluted organisational politics, enigmatic communication patterns, idiosyncratic management styles and oppressive rules and regulations (Hickman and Lee, 2001). A review of the factors associated with stress (Michie, 2002) identified a number of key areas such as long hours worked, overload and pressure, exclusion from decision-making, poor social support, ambiguous work role and poor management style.

There is evidence to suggest that these general stressors are compounded by one's occupation. A review of the labour force in Sweden showed that the professional categories showing the highest proportion of stress-related disorders were social work and psychology (Tham, 2006). A study of stress experienced by mental health social workers revealed that forty-seven per cent indicated a possible psychological disorder with a further fifty-five per cent indicating a probable mental disorder (Huxley et al., 2005). Collins (2008) asserts that the particular demands made of child care social workers in social service settings contributes to them experiencing more stress, less job satisfaction and difficulty in coping. Similarly, Coffey et al. (2004) found the highest levels of sickness and mental distress among child care social workers.

As a professional group, social workers have few intermediaries between themselves and their client group and, as such, undertake high levels of emotional labour (Johnson et al., 2005). However, unlike other professions that are similarly exposed, such as teachers and nurses, social workers' clientele comes mainly from groups where there are high levels of need and social exclusion (Jones, 2001). Regular exposure to severely abused or neglected children can feel similar to being in a war zone (Azar, 2000). Exposure to direct and indirect trauma, and exposure to multi-stressed families typically seen in child protection work, is an obvious drain on practitioners. Azar cites Figley (1995) who defined such exhaustion as 'compassion fatigue'. Such vicarious traumatisation is a well recognised occupational hazard that is closely associated with burnout. Burnout has been described as having three sub-dimensions: emotional exhaustion, depersonalisation (negative feelings and cynicism) and a sense of reduced personal accomplishment in one's work (Maslach and Jackson, 1981; Westbrook et al., 2006).

A study undertaken by Stanley et al. (2006) found that while some social workers had downgraded to posts without management responsibilities, others chose to move into management positions to escape the demands of face-to-face work with clients. Others opt to leave altogether. In Tham's study (2006) of social workers in child welfare, forty-eight per cent described themselves as fairly likely, or very likely, to look for a new job within the year. The main reason for leaving was volume of work, role conflicts and exposure to threats and violence.

Yet not everyone leaves. Despite the hazards, studies show that there is an intrinsically high level of job satisfaction within the care workforce generally (Cameron, 2003).

Reasons for staying

There are a number of identifiable, key reasons why staff choose to stay even when the going is tough. Essentially these are commitment to their mission, professional loyalty and personal resilience.

Commitment

In a survey of over 1,400 child welfare workers in Georgia, USA, Ellett *et al.* (2003) identified a professional commitment to child welfare as the main reason of intent to remain employed in child welfare work. According to a study conducted in the United Kingdom (Rose, 2003), social workers were in the top twenty occupations that enjoyed job satisfaction. Despite all the work pressures there is plenty of evidence that social workers are committed to the work they do and motivated by the belief that they can make a real difference to the lives of clients (McLean and Andrew, 2000; Eborall and Garmeson, 2001; Huxley *et al.*, 2005; Collins, 2008).

Commenting on the work of Coffey *et al.* (2004), which found that 4.1 per cent of social workers were on sick leave as a result of stress, Collins (2008) asks: 'What about the 95.9 per cent who were not off work as a result of stress?' In this regard Westbrook *et al.* (2006) refer to these as 'committed survivors' who are characteristically calmer, less emotionally charged and more reflective that others in similar situations.

The characteristics that 'committed survivors' believe are essential for remaining employed in a public child welfare setting are:

- Efficient time management and organisational skills.
- An open, non-judgemental, attitude.
- Self-confidence.
- Personal commitment (to clients and the larger profession).
- Compassion combined with firmness.
- Intuition (thinking on one's feet).
- Strong self-efficacy beliefs.
- Ability to be a team player and yet be able to work independently.
- Ability to 'make your needs known'.
- Enjoyment of problem solving.
- Keeping things in perspective.
- Balancing the demands of work and one's personal life.

(Westbrook *et al.*, 2006)

The commitment of workers can be closely associated with professional vocation. It is also much more likely to occur in organisations where there is harmony in relation to organisational mission and purpose. Organisational commitment is achieved when members of staff accept the organisational goals and values; are willing to help the organisation achieve them; and have a desire to remain with the organisation.

Professional loyalty

Professional loyalty is a powerful motivation for social workers to keep going. From the study undertaken by Huxley *et al.* (2005), it was concluded that workers were staying not necessarily because they share the goals and values of the employer organisation, but because of a professional commitment to the goals and values of their profession and to the service users. Most social care workers are trained to be advocates for their clients. They have a dual loyalty to their organisation and their profession (Austin, 2002). It is vitally important that managers recognise and work with this professional energy if they are to avoid social workers becoming an 'independent republic' within the organisation. Napoleon is reputed to have said: 'I fight with my soldiers' dreams'. Taking such a leadership approach is much more likely to bring results than bellowing instructions (Harrison, 2006). Vocation is a massive natural resource for managers to harness and nurture as it can contribute hugely to staff welfare and, consequently, to better client outcomes.

Resilience

Clarke (2007, 2008) has developed ways of enhancing the resilience of people in high risk jobs; she suggests that the key to high performance is to manage one's energy not one's time.

The key to managing successful energy is the balancing of expenditure and recovery across four domains:
1. Being physically energised – this can be assisted by recovery breaks to sustain performance.
2. Being emotionally connected – the experience of enjoyment, challenge, adventure and opportunity are key to well-being.
3. Being mentally focused – using mental capacity to focus attention and avoid rumination.
4. Being spiritually aligned – balancing a commitment beyond one's self with adequate self-care.

Finally, a general point worthy of note is that a modicum of staff attrition is not necessarily a bad thing. For example, it can provide managers with opportunities to refresh teams, or to try new things with new people. Teams that remain static in composition are at serious risk of remaining static in thought as well.

Reasons for leaving

There are essentially three primary reasons why staff decide to throw in the towel: the perceived burden of national policy and performance initiatives; adverse organisational culture; and the stress and threat of violence. Contrary to common perception, it is bureaucratic rigour and adverse management styles that are more likely to be the straw that breaks the camel's back than the threatening behaviour of service users. However, each has its own distinct features and is, therefore, discussed separately.

The perceived burden of national policy and performance initiatives

Rose *et al.* (2007) ask:

> What happens when pristine policies, clear in its objectives and proposals for delivery and fully supported by all relevant stakeholders, leaves the hands of central government policy makers and becomes the responsibility of local government authorities or service providing agencies . . .

The answer, they suggest, is often huge disappointment in the hearts of these policy makers at the apparent failure of others to implement their best intentions.

There is evidence to show that Government policy and the administrative demands that flow from it, actually contribute to the stress levels of workers (Huxley *et al.*, 2005). Typically these demands are associated statutory responsibilities that require an inordinate amount of form-filling, which is not viewed as particularly relevant by practitioners, but is seen as a distraction from face-to-face work with service users and other core professional activities. This point has been reiterated by Munro (2008), commenting upon the circumstances surrounding the death of Baby P in Haringey. She asserts that the Government's efforts to improve child protection since the Climbié report has been misdirected, resulting in too much emphasis being placed on administrative accountability and not enough on face-to-face work with children and families.

Waves of legislation and associated policies and procedures have been perceived (Jones, 2001) as a 'regulatory intrusion', resulting in social service departments being far less involved in the provision of services and far more involved in the gate-keeping and the policing of services. This has the knock-on effect of altering social work practice, much to the frustration of practitioners. According to Jones (2001) current Government initiatives are replacing traditional public service orientations with the logic of hard-nosed commercialism: the preoccupation with monitoring people as well as activity is creating what he calls a 'tagged society'.

With all the information now being collected, ostensibly in the name of management, there is little evidence that it is being put to good use. The separation of practice information on individual children and families from aggregated data required by managers results in Government returns having little or nothing to do with the overall business of service delivery (Ward, 2004). As alluded to in Chapter 6, the issue for managers is not so much the collection of data *per se*, but the interpretation of it in order to gain insights that can enhance knowledge or translate findings into positive action for the betterment of children and families (Ward, 2004).

Adverse organisational culture

The context for statutory social work is changing. This is evident from the joining together of children's services and education in England, together with closer ties to services for adults (Collins, 2008). It is also evident in Ireland with the move towards Primary Care Teams that will bring social workers into much closer alliances with medical, paramedical and nursing professions (HSE, 2007). Patterns of constant change have been identified as a stressor in a large proportion of staff (Jones, 2001; Stanley et al., 2007; Devine, 2007).

In a survey, nearly sixty per cent of social workers identified work as the most frequent cause of depression, while others cited a lack of control or the absence of boundaries as a contributory factor (Stanley et al., 2002). Jones (2001) found that as much as ninety per cent of community social workers' time was being taken up with what was described as 'bureaucracy and paperwork'. This inevitably leads to less direct work with service users; a situation also observed by Huxley et al. (2005).

Recurring themes identified by Tham (2007) included supervision, support and feedback which, when lacking or absent, adversely affect worker well-being. Lack of organisational support and the effects of bureaucratisation in the structures of child protection organisations have been identified (Stanley and Goddard, 2002) as having an alienating effect on staff. As such the divisions between staff and management become more stark (Jones, 2001).

Another organisational pressure was identified as the additional burden to exiting staff from staff absences and vacancies. In Ireland, the Health Service Executive, as a cost-cutting measure, took a decision that, as from a particular date, any vacant social work posts would simply be expunged.

Westbrook et al. (2006) describe the familiar scenario (see Chapter 3) whereby the death of a child invoked in the organisation a response typified by rigid policies and procedures, heightened monitoring and accountability without the provision of resources that were required to reduce caseloads, uncompensated after-hours work, and improved supervision arrangements. It is bad enough when a hierarchical, bureaucratic, organisational structure is neutral on the issue of worker well-being but it becomes entirely destructive when an organisation is driven by a blame culture that allows individuals to be hung out to dry in favour of organisational self-preservation while underlying systemic failures remain unaddressed. Jones (2001) found opinions being expressed that many managers had lost touch with the welfare ideals of social work. One social worker expressed amazement that an agency that is supposed to be so attuned to the impact of life events on people, could be so unaware of the needs of staff.

Tham (2007) found that what she refers to as the 'human resource orientation' of an organisation was of major importance. That is to say, the extent to which members of staff were rewarded for a job well done, felt well taken care of, and where management showed an interest in the health and well-being, were very significant contributors to staff retention.

As has been referred to in the Introduction to this book, there is evidence to suggest that the way in which child welfare and protection services are managed has altered greatly in recent years. The familiar ways of traditional supervision methods, expounded by Kadushin (1992) and Morrison (1999) among others have, if not given way to, at least been appended by, new management tasks. There is, arguably, a risk that front line managers must inevitably reduce the original purpose of supervision (accountability, support and development) to a more restrictive version that is primarily concerned with performance management. As such, the original emphasis of supervision shifts from support for the individual worker to mechanisms that gauge the quality of the organisational performance (Jones and Gallop, 2003; Statham, 2004). An unintended consequence of this is that many people in the worst affected agencies vote with their feet.

Stanley and Goddard (2002) found that in a strongly bureaucratic structure, satisfaction with feedback on work issues decreased as the bureaucratic level got higher. This results in workers becoming alienated from management and team members resort to supplying a self-sufficient style of support to each other: staff build a psychological wall between the team and the rest of the organisation and exist in a self-made cocoon. In effect, they become uncommitted to the organisation as a whole.

The stress and threat of violence

The possibility of violence and aggression tends to come with the territory as part of the social work task. It can be understood as a reflection of the stress service users' experience which, in turn, can be associated with broader issues concerned with social exclusion (Thompson *et al.*, 1994). Social work must deal with a range of unpleasant things arising from such exclusion and deprivation. Many service users will have experienced and internalised a process of dehumanisation, having experienced being treated as 'inanimate' objects of violence and external abuse (Davies, 1998) and, as a result, will seek to punish others.

Unlike other aspects of state social policy provision, such as health and education, social work is much more class specific (Jones, 2001). This is particularly so in the areas of child protection which, as discussed in Chapter 3, tends to be linked with areas of high deprivation. This contrasts, for example, with social work in the hospice movement, which, although stressful by nature, is non class-specific and non-violent. In addition, child protection work relies heavily on home visitation as a means of engagement with families. There are many inherent risks associated with this, where workers have to enter dangerous neighbourhoods and hostile homes. In such situations even subtle forms of intimidation can leave workers feeling very vulnerable indeed.

The stress associated with the threat or actuality of violent behaviour is not diminished by frequent exposure. The more a worker experiences threats of violence, the more they perceive the threat of assault as a major source of stress (Jones *et al.*, 1991). In this case, familiarity does not breed contempt. Insufficient attention is given to the effects of violence on social work practice. Some workers have expressed the view that management has failed to acknowledge the level of concern among some workers who were exposed to serious incidents or psychological violence on a regular basis (Stanley and Goddard, 2002).

Lack of organisational support is a reality for many staff. Davies (1998) suggests that some social work organisations are structured in such a way as to push most junior staff into front-line work. Stanley and Goddard (2002) found that, while seventy per cent of workers believed their immediate supervisors would provide automatic support, twenty-one per cent believed that 'head office' would not; and, in fact, many believed that they would be blamed if an adverse incident occurred.

There is little doubt that bureaucratic organisations are less responsive to staff requirements and, as such, tend to minimise corporate responsibilities to staff. In such an environment departments work to serve their own function with no meaningful linkages to other departments. Decisions are taken at the top with little insight into their implications; front line works are not consulted; and little recognition is given to those working face-to-face with the service user. The knock-on effect is that front line staff feel excluded; back room staff feel no connection to the service user and management is not trusted or respected (MacDonald, 2003). In effect, the system becomes heartless.

What managers can do for staff

There is a requirement for managers to proactively affect the mood of the workforce in a positive manner. This is an ongoing battle that is pitched against other legitimate forces such as professional loyalty, the personal needs of workers and organisational insensitivity. This organisational insensitivity is not necessary intentionally constructed by particular people at the top; rather it is the unintended consequence of an imperfect system that fails to sufficiently recognise the worth of individuals.

Middle managers, in particular, have a responsibility to seek to rectify this imperfection by bridging the gap between senior management and workers at the front line. A measure of success in this regard is the size of the gap between 'us' (the workers) and 'them' (management). In the most successful organisations there will only be 'us', where common values and a clear sense of vision and mission are shared by all within an agreed purpose for the organisation. The work performed must be meaningful to the employee as well as the organisation. These goals are interactive, reciprocal and, sometimes contradictory (Browne, 2000) so they require proactive and dynamic management.

In seeking this organisational nirvana managers need to be conscious of the values and underlying principles from which they are working, the part they have to play in achieving it, and the practical steps that are required to reach it.

Management values and principles

Chapter 1 discusses how values and ethics are the cornerstones of good practice. Suffice it to say here, in the context of the management of practice, that what is good or bad, right or wrong, about a management decision depends on the ethical and moral principles that are taken into consideration; what values are held important; who might be affected by the decision; and what price one is prepared to pay for it (Hickman and Lee, 2001). In this regard managers should hark back to the basic principles of the reformers from years gone by and re-examine the heritage of public service. Managers must continue to exhibit professionalism, promote merit and ensure accountability to political leaders and avoid the pitfalls of partisan bias (Berman *et al.*, 2005).

Respect for the person is at the heart of person-centred management and, as such, it is well suited to human service management. Person-centred management creates a new culture that encourages employees to actively participate and to think creatively. It promotes a culture of positive management where people are involved in problem-solving and decision-making, a culture of ownership where people see themselves as partners and have a strong sense of responsibility and commitment to the organisation (Browne, 2005). Employee-friendly policies can also lead to important positive outcomes for staff, such as improved job satisfaction, reduced absenteeism, productivity, better morale, retention and loyalty.

Implications for managers

The work undertaken by Westbrook *et al.* (2006) highlighted the importance of local management. Staff spoke of the need for professional and personal support from managers. Local managers and administrators were viewed as flexible and understanding, acting as a buffer between their work in the local agency and the demands and criticisms from the state (head office). This higher level was considered by front line staff as making bureaucratic, self-serving demands that were out of touch with work-place realities and unresponsive to client need. However, the scenario in this US study could not only be imported to Western Europe, but could also be put to music, such is its resonance with the status quo closer to home.

Yet these stereotypical attitudes should not be left unattended and, where appropriate, unchallenged. Social workers, in particular, are good at circling the wagons, viewing themselves as being at the centre, lacking the necessary resources for survival and under siege from external forces, including senior managers. This is not a healthy situation if it exists. It re-enforces the role of the middle managers in bridging the gap between senior management and front line staff.

According to Westbrook *et al.* (2006), the implications for upper management is that they should formulate policies that allow staff to rotate assignments from time to time; that they need to arrange for reasonable workloads and, by creating dual career paths, improve staff retention by facilitating experienced staff who want to stay at practitioner level. However a more fundamental response might be to take a leaf from what worked for local managers. The simple act of taking time to listen to 'war stories' and the provision of informal feedback in relation to persistence, effort and successes was hugely reinforcing for front line staff. Therefore, a simple phone call from a senior manager to a first-line worker who had a traumatic experience or a notable success would work wonders for morale and provide a boost for the workforce generally. Conversely, the absence of such a call supports employee belief that they are under-valued and under-supported by senior management in the work they do. Even generals pin medals on fallen soldiers.

Military style language abounds in child protection work in particular. One talks of 'front-line workers', 'in the trenches', 'over the top', 'under siege' and 'them' (management) as if they were a hostile force. But who is the enemy? Perhaps it is the misunderstanding experienced by staff at all levels of the role and the needs of other members of staff at different levels. Therefore, concepts such as diplomacy, conciliation and peace-making need to be engaged as a means of ensuring that management and staff can join forces in a mission that will achieve the ultimate victory: better outcomes for service users as a result of the services provided.

Practical steps managers can take to improve staff well-being

Considerations for first line managers might include:

1. Supervision
   Good, traditional supervision in sufficient frequency is the perfect tonic for staff well-being and professional development. It should not, as discussed above, be substituted as a management tool for performance measurement. Of course, supervision must be responsive to the needs of individual employees; hand-holding may not be enough and managers may be required to actively do something to make a difference. According to Azar (2000): 'Working with individual practitioners in supervision . . . without changing some of the realities of their work would be like arguing for the value of therapy for sexually abused children, without protecting them from the offender.'

2. Realistic expectations
   One goal in supervision might usefully be to provide the supervisee with a revised view of the world that is more in line with the realities of the work; a view that allows them to retain meaning for themselves in the face of many obstacles to feeling successful. Just as recovery for the patient is not a goal for the social worker in a hospice setting, realistic expectations in child welfare and protection work are equally important. The supervisor can reduce stress by helping supervisees to negotiate clear expectations with all parties at the outset. Clear expectations, in terms that are workable, provide a sense of safety that is crucial in work that can be traumatic in nature (Azar, 2000).

3. Monitoring risk
   Supervision has the capacity to develop clear strategies to deal with risk issues. The level of danger should be monitored and situations that are too dangerous should be identified and avoided (Azar, 2000). In particular, the benefit of the home visit, a feature of child protection work, need to be weighed against the safety of the worker.

4. Coping strategies
   Coping strategies involve planning for how a stress might be coped with and coming up with strategies to handle it. 'Vigilant coping' is aimed at problem-solving, or doing something to avoid, prevent or control the stress. 'Emotional-focused coping' is aimed at managing the emotional distress associated with a particular situation, rather than dealing with the stressor itself (Collins, 2008).

5. On-site training
   On the job training was identified (Westbrook *et al.*, 2006) as the greatest contribution to strengthening retention and improving the competence of new workers, more so

than formalised education. Strategies must be developed for recognising good practice at the level of the individual worker, the team and the organisation. Also, individual workers need to take responsibility to access ongoing professional development in a variety of forms (Gordon, 2007; Buckley *et al.*, 2008).

Considerations for senior management might include:
1. Workforce planning
   To date most senior management attention has been focused on recruitment strategies and the timely filling of vacancies. However, unless retention forms part of the strategy, the effect will simply be to create a younger workforce that burns out earlier (Stanley *et al.*, 2007).
   Consideration also needs to be given to curricula in higher level institutions because it cannot be assumed that newly qualified social workers and social care workers come fully equipped to 'hit the ground running' in a child welfare and protection environment. As well as skills in child protection, consideration might also be given by educators to understanding the workings of large bureaucracies and the development of skills to navigate barriers, resolve conflicts and negotiate solutions (Westbrook *et al.*, 2006).
2. Support:
   Employers of choice are those with a policy to ensure regular, quality supervision to staff. Senior management, as well as line managers, need to be sensitive to issues of worker safety and aware of the stresses associated with child protection work. This can be addressed at a fundamental level by the development of policies concerning staff health, well-being and safety. At a more creative level it might include the formal recognition of work well done through modest recognition awards or letters of commendation.
3. Working conditions
   At an organisational level there needs to be a strategy in place for determining what an acceptable workload level is and for the management and distribution of high-risk cases. Strategies for dealing with excessive workloads also need to be developed, and this may involve alerting the political system to unresolved difficulties in this regard. Unnecessary paperwork should be scraped and necessary paperwork should be presented to practitioners in the form of messages that assist practice.
4. Clinical governance
   Much emphasis has been placed on the responsibility of workers to produce information data to managers and on managers to use it as a means of measuring performance. However, little attention has been paid to how professions might govern themselves. There is a glimmer of hope in Ireland currently, where the Health Service Executive is considering the development of Clinical Director posts where practitioners would be responsible for the development, leadership and monitoring of their own professional services. It can only be advantageous to invest this level of responsibility in the professions where the knowledge rests (Harrison, 2008).

Main Messages

- An effective way to satisfy staff is to find out what they want and, to the extent possible, give it to them.
- Staff stay because of their commitment, professional loyalty and personal resilience.
- Staff leave because of bureaucratic rigor and adverse management styles more so than the stress and threat of violence.
- Respect for the person is at the heart of person-centred management.
- Good supervision is the perfect tonic for staff well-being and development and should not be substituted as a management tool for performance measurement.

References

Adams, K. (2001) *Developing Quality to Protect Children: SSI Inspection of Children's Services, August 1999–July 2000.* London: SSI.

Adams, R. (1998) *Quality Social Work.* Basingstoke: Macmillan.

Affolter, F.W. (2005) Socio-Emotional Enablement and the Convention of the Rights of the Child. *The International Journal of Children's Rights,* 13: 379–97.

Ainsworth, F. and Hansen, P. (2006) Five Tumultuous Years in Australian Child Protection: Little Progress. *Child and Family Social Work,* 11: 33–41.

Ashworth, R., Boyne, G.A., McGarvey, N. and Walker, R.M. (2002) Regulating Public Bodies: The Case of Direct Service Organisations in British Local Government. *Environment and Planning C; Government and Policy,* 20, 455–70.

Austin, D. (2002) *Human Service Management: Organisational Leadership in Social Work Practice.* New York: Columbia University Press.

Axford, N. and Little, M. (2005) Refocusing Children's Services Towards Prevention: Lessons from the Literature. *Children and Society,* 20: 299–312.

Azar, S. (2000) Preventing Burnout in Professional and Paraprofessionals who Work with Child Abuse and Neglect Cases: A Cognitive Behavioural Approach to Supervision. *Psychology in Practice,* 56: 5, 643–63.

Ball, C. (1998) Regulating Child Care: From the Children Act 1948 to the Present Day. *Child and Family Social Work,* 3: 163–71.

Beckett, C. (2003) *Child Protection: An Introduction.* London: Sage.

Beecham, J. and Sinclair, I. (2007) *Costs and Outcomes in Children's Social Care: Messages from Research.* London: Jessica Kingsley.

Behn, R.D. (2003) Why Measure Performance? Different Purposes Require Different Measures. *Public Administration Review.* 63: 5.

Bell, M. (1995) A Study of the Attitudes of Nurses to Parental Involvement in the Initial Child Protection Conference and their Preparation for it. *Journal of Advanced Nursing,* 22: 250–57.

Bell, M. (1999) Working in Partnership in Child Protection: The Conflicts. *British Journal of Social Work,* 29, 437–55.

Bell, M. and Wilson, K. (2006) Research Note: Children's Views of Family Group Conferences. *British Journal of Social Work,* 36: 671–81.

Bell. M. (2004) Child Protection at the Community Level. *Child Abuse Review.* 13: 363–67.

Benatar, D. (2006) *Cutting to the Core: Exploring the Ethics of Contested Surgeries.* Lanham, MD: Rowan and Littlefield.

Beresford, P. (2001) Critical Commentaries: Service Users. *British Journal of Social Work,* 31, 629–30.

Beresford, P. and Croft, S. (2004) Service Users and Practitioners Reunited: The Key Component for Social Work Reform. *British Journal of Social Work,* 34, 53–68.

Berman, E.M. *et al.* (2005) *Human Resource Management in Public Service: Paradoxes, Processes and Problems.* 2nd edn. Thousand Oaks: Sage.

Berridge, D. and Brodie, I. (1998) *Children's Homes Revisited.* Jessica Kingsley.

Berry, M., Charlson, R. and Dawson, K. (2003) Promising Practices in Understanding and Treating Child Neglect. *Child and Family Social Work,* 8, 13–24.

Bessant, J., and Hil, R. (2005) Abuse of Young People in Australia and the Conditions for Restoring Public Trust. In Bessant, J., Hil, R. and Watts, R. (Eds.) *Violations of Trust: How Social and Welfare Institutions Fail Children and Young People.* Aldershot: Ashgate.

Beveridge, W. (1942) *Social Insurance and Allied Services*. London: HMSO.
Biestek, F. (1961) *The Casework Relationship*. London: Allen and Unwin.
Booker, O. (2008) *The Manager's Mentor: A Practical Companion and Guide to Managing Yourself and Others in the Human Services*. Lyme Regis: Russell House Publishing.
Booth, C. (1889) *Life and Labour of the People of London*. London: Macmillan.
Bosnich, D. (1996) The Principle of Subsidiarity. *Religion and Liberty*, 6: 4.
Bowlby, J. (1969) *Attachment and Loss*. New York: Basic Books. British Association of Social Workers www.basw.co.uk (Accessed May 1st, 2008).
Britton, C. and Esquibel-Hunt, D. (2004) *Helping in Child Protective Services: A Competency-based Casework Handbook*. New York: Oxford University Press.
Brown, L. (2003) Mainstream or Margin? The Current Use of Family Group Conferences in Child Welfare Practice in the UK. *Child and Family Social Work*, 8: 311–40.
Browne, D. (2000) *Keeping Resources Human: A Practical Guide to Retaining Staff*. Cork: Onstream Publications.
Buckley, H. (2002) *Child Protection and Welfare: Innovations and Interventions*. Dublin: Institute of Public Administration.
Buckley, H. (2003) *Child Protection Work: Beyond the Rhetoric*. London: Jessica Kingsley.
Buckley, H. (2007) Differential Responses to Child Protection Reports. *Irish Journal of Family Law*. 3.
Buckley, H., Whelan, S., Carr, N. and Murphy, C. (2008) *Service Users' Perceptions of the Irish Child Protection System*. Dublin: Office of the Minister for Children and Youth Affairs.
Buckley, H., Horwath, J. and Whelan, S. (2006) *Framework for the Assessment of Vulnerable Children and their Families*. Dublin: Children's Research Centre, Trinity College.
Buckley, H., Skehill, C. and O'Sullivan, E. (1997) *Child Protection Practices in Ireland: A Case Study*. Dublin: Oak Tree Press.
Calder, M.C. (1995) Child Protection: Balancing Paternalism and Partnership. *British Journal of Social Work*, 25: 749–66.
Calder, M.C. (2002) A Framework for Conducting Risk Assessment. *Child Care in Practice*, 8: 1.
Calder, M.C. and Hackett, S. (2003) *The Assessment Framework: A Critique and Reformulation*. In *Assessment in Child Care: Using and Developing Frameworks for Practice*. Lyme Regis: Russell House Publishing.
Calder, M.C. (2007) (Ed.) *Contemporary Risk Assessment in Safeguarding Children*. Lyme Regis: Russell House Publishing.
Calder, M.C. (2007) Child Protection: The Manager's Perspective. In *The Child Protection Handbook*. 3rd edn. London: Balliere Tindall.
Cameron, C. (2003) *Care Work and Care Workers* in *Social Care Workforce Research: Needs and Priorities*. London: Social Care Workforce Research Unit, King's College.
Cameron, G., Vanderwoerd, J. and Peirson, L. (1997) *Protecting Children and Supporting Families: Promising Programmes and Organisational Realities*. 2nd edn. New York: Aldine.
Campbell, P. (1996) The History of the User Movement in the United Kingdom. In Heller, T. *et al.* (Eds.) *Mental Health Matters*. Basingstoke: Macmillan.
Carter, N., Klein, R. and Day, P. (1992) *How Organisations Measure Success*. London: Routledge.
Cheetham, J., Fuller, R., McIvor, G. and Petch, A. (1992) *Evaluating Social Work Effectiveness*. Buckingham: Open University.
Chief Inspector (2005) *Safeguarding Children: Second Report of the Joint Chief Inspectors' Report on Arrangements to Safeguard Children*. London: Commission of Social Care Inspection.
Child Welfare League of America (1996) *Standards of Excellence: CWLA Standards of Excellence for the Management and Governance of Child Welfare Organizations*. Washington DC: CWLA.
Child Welfare League of America (1999) *Standards of Excellence: CWLA Standards of Excellence for Services for Abused or Neglected Children and their Families*. Revised Edn. Washington, DC: CWLA.
Child, Youth and Family (2007) *Leading for Outcomes*. New Zealand: Child, Youth and Family.

Children's Rights Director (2004) *Safe from Harm: Children's Views Report.* London: Commission of Social Care Inspection.

Children's Rights Director (2004) *Safe from Harm: Children's Views Report.* London: Commission of Social Care Inspection.

Clark, C.L. (2000) *Social Work Ethics: Principles and Practice.* London: Palgrave.

Clark, C. (2005) Moral Character in Social Work, *British Journal of Social Work,* 36, 75–89.

Clarke, J. (2007) *Enhancing Resilience in High Risk Jobs: Self Care Skills and Strategies.* Keynote address to the National Association for the Treatment of Abusers, March 30th, 2007. Malahide Co. Dublin.

Clarke, J. (2008) Promoting Professional Resilience. In Calder, M. (Ed.) *Contemporary Risk Assessment in Safeguarding Children.* Lyme Regis: Russell House Publishing.

Cleaver, H. and Freeman, P. (1995) *Parental Perspectives in Cases of Suspected Child Abuse.* London: HMSO.

Cliffe, D. with Berridge, D. (1992) *Closing Children's Homes: An End to Residential Childcare?* London: NCB.

Coffey, M., Dugdill, L. and Tattersall, A. (2004) Research Note: Stress in Social Services: Mental Well-being, Constraints and Job Satisfaction. *British Journal of Social Work,* 34: 5, 735–47.

Collins, M. (2006) The Children Order: A Perspective from the United States. *Child Care in Practice,* 12: 2, 113–27.

Collins, S. (2008) Statutory Social Workers: Stress, Job Satisfaction, Coping, Social Support and Individual Differences. *British Journal of Social Work,* 38: 1173–93.

Commission for Social Care Inspection (2005) *Making Social Care Better for People.* London: CSCI.

Commission to Inquire into Child Abuse (2003) *3rd Interim Report.* Dublin: CICA.

Connolly, M. (2007*) DRM New Zealand Style: Practicing for Outcomes, Supporting Rights and Changing Lives.* Keynote address to the American Humane Conference on the Differential Response Model. Los Angeles, CA, November 14–17.

Connolly, M. and Doolan, M. (2007) Responding to the Deaths of Children Known to Child Protection Agencies. *Social Policy Journal of New Zealand,* 30.

Co-operation and Working Together (2008) *Literature Review for Framework for Integrated Planning for Outcomes for Children and Families.* Armagh: CAWT www.cawt.com (Accessed April 28th, 2008)

Corby, B. (1987) *Working with Child Abuse.* Milton Keynes: Open University Press.

Corby, B. (2006) *Child Abuse: Towards a Knowledge Base.* 3rd edn. Maidenhead: Open University.

Corby, B. (2006) The Role of Child Care Social Work in Supporting Families with Children in Need and Providing Protective Services – Past, Present and Future. *Child Abuse Review,* 15: 159–77.

Corby, B., Doig, A. and Roberts, V. (2001) *Public Inquiries into Abuse of Children in Residential Care* London: Jessica Kingsley.

Coulton, C., Crampton, D., Irwan, M., Spilsbury, J. and Korbin, J. (2007) How Neighborhoods Influence Child Maltreatment: A Review of the Literature. *Child Abuse and Neglect,* 31; 1117–42.

Council of Europe (1996) *European Social Charter* www.coe.int (Accessed November 3rd 2008).

Crimmens, D. (2000) Things Can Only Get Better! An Evaluation of Developments in the Training and Qualification of Residential Child Care Staff. In Crimmens, D. and Pitts, J. (Eds.) *Positive Residential Practice: Learning the Lessons of the 1990s.* Lyme Regis: Russell House Publishing.

Croft, S., Adshead, L. and Bersford, P. (2004) *The Involve Project: What Service Users Want from Specialist Palliative Care Social Work.* York: York Publishing.

Cuddenback, G. (2004) Kinship Family Foster Care: A Methodological and Substantive Synthesis of Research. *Children and Youth Services Review,* 26: 7, 623–39.

Cullen, B. (1998) *Social Partnerships and Children's Services.* Dublin: Children's Research Centre, Trinity College.

Culpitt, I. (1999) *Social Policy and Risk.* London: Sage.

Cunningham, G. (2004) Supervision and Governance. In Statham, D. (Ed.) *Managing Front Line Practice in Social Care.* London: Jessica Kingsley.

Dale, P. (2004) 'Like a Fish in a Bowl': Parents' Perceptions of Child Protection Services. *Child Abuse Review*, 13: 137–57.

Daniel, P. and Ivatts, J. (1998) *Children and Social Policy*. London: Macmillan.

Darro, D. and Donnelly, A.C. (2002) Charting the Waves of Prevention: Two Steps Forward, One Step Back. *Child Abuse and Neglect*, 26: 731–42.

Dartington Social Research Unit (1995) *Child Protection: Messages from Research*. London: HMSO.

Davies, S. (2004) Power and Knowledge: The Making and Maintaining of the 'Unfit'. In Bessant, J., Hill, R. and Watts, R. (Eds.) *Violations of Trust: How Social and Welfare Institutions Fail Children and Young People*. Aldershot: Ashgate.

Davis, L. (2004) The Difference Between Child Abuse and Child Protection Could Be You: Creating a Community Network of Protective Adults. *Child Abuse Review*, 13: 426–32.

Davies, R. (Ed.) (1998) *Stress in Social Work*. London: Jessica Kingsley.

Dawson, A. and Butler, B. (2003) The Morally Active Manager. In Henderson, J. and Atkinson, D. (Eds.) *Managing Care in Context*. London: Routledge.

De la Harpe, D., Kavanagh, P. and Turner, M. (2008) Beware: What Gets Measured Might Just Get Done. *Health Manager, Journal of the Health Management Institute of Ireland*. April/May.

Department of Child Youth and Family Services (2007) *Leading for Outcomes: Strategic Direction for 2007–2010*. Wellington: Child Youth and Family.

Department of Education and Skills (2006) *Care Matters: Transforming the Lives of Children and Young People in Care*. London: DES.

Department of Education and Skills (2006) *Referrals, Assessment and Children and Young People on Child Protection Registers, England*. London: DES.

Department of Health (1995) *Child Protection: Messages from Research*. London: HMSO.

Department of Health (1998) *Modernising Social Services: Promoting Independence, Improving Protection, Raising Standards*. London: HMSO.

Department of Health (1999) *Working Together to Safeguard Children: A Guide to Inter-Agency Working to Safeguard and Promote the Welfare of Children*. London: HMSO.

Department of Health (2000) *Framework for the Assessment of Children in Need and their Families*. London: HMSO.

Department of Health (2003) *Children Looked After by Local Authorities, Year Ending 31 March 2002*. London: HMSO.

Department of Health (2003) *Social Services Performance Assessment Framework Indicators 2001–2002*. London: HMSO.

Department of Health and Children (1999*) Children First: National Guidelines for the Protection and Welfare of Children*. Dublin: Government Publications.

Department of Health and Children (2000) *National Children's Strategy*. Dublin: Government Publications.

Department of Health and Children (2003) *Working for Children and Families: Exploring Good Practice*. Dublin: Government Publications.

Department of Health and Children (2006) *State of the Nation's Children*. Dublin: DoH&C.

Department of Health and Children (2007) *The Agenda for Children's Services: A Policy Handbook*. Dublin: Office of the Minister for Children.

Department of Health, Social Service Inspectorate (1995) *The Challenge of Partnership in Child Protection: Practice Guide*. London: HMSO.

Department for Innovation, Universities and Skills (2007) *Children Looked After by Local Authorities, Year Ending 31 March 2004– 2006*. London: HMSO.

Department of Social and Family Affairs (1998) *The Commission on the Family Report*. Dublin: Government Publications.

Devine, C. (2007) The Best Way to Implement Reform. *Health Manager: Journal of the Health Management Institute of Ireland*, August, 22–4.

Dickens, J. *et al.* (2007) Children Starting to be Looked After by Local Authorities in England: An Analysis of Inter-authority Variation and Case-centred Decision Making. *British Journal of Social Work*, 37, 597–617.

Dickens, J., Howell, D., Thoburn, J., Schofield, G., Dingwall, R., Eekekaar, J. and Murray, T. (1983) *The Protection of Children: State Intervention and Family Life*. Oxford: Blackwell.

Dingwall, R., Eekekaar, J. and Murray, T. *Protection of Children*. Oslo: NOROS

Dinnage, R. and Kellmer Pringle, M.C. (1965) *Residential Child Care: Facts and Fallacies*. London: Longman.

Dolan, P., Canavan, J. and Pinkerton, J. (2006) Family Support: From Description to Reflection. In Dolan, P., Canavan, J. and Pinkerton, J. *Family Support as a Reflective Practice*. London: Jessica Kingsley.

Drucker, P.F. (1990) *Managing the Non-profit Organisation: Priorities and Principles*. London: Butterworth-Heineman.

Eborall, C. and Garmeson, K. (2001) *Desk Research on Recruitment and Retention in Social Care and Social Work*. London: Business and Industrial Market Research.

Ellett, A.J., Ellett, C.D and Rugutt, J.K. (2003) *A Study of Personal and Organizational Factors Contributing to Employee Retention and Turnover in Child Welfare in Georgia*. Athens, GA: University of Georgia, School of Social Work.

English, D.J. and Pecora, P.J. (1994) Risk Assessment as a Practice Method in Child Protective Services. *Child Welfare*, 73: 5, 451–73.

European Union (1996) *European Social Charter*. Strasbourg: Council of Europe.

Farmer, E. and Owen, M. (1995) *Child Protection Practice: Private Risks and Public Remedies*. London: HMSO.

Farmer, E. and Pollock, S. (1999) Mix and Match: Planning to Keep Looked-after Children Safe. *Child Abuse Review*, 8: 377–91.

Fattore, T., Mason, J. and Watson, E. (2007) Children's Conceptualization(s) of their Well-being. *Journal of Social Indicators Research*, 80. 5–29.

Ferguson, H. (1996) Protecting Irish Children in Time: Child Abuse as a Social Problem and the Development of the Child Protection System in the Republic of Ireland. *Administration*, 44: 2, 5–36.

Ferguson, H. (2004) *Protecting Children in Time: Child Abuse, Child Protection and the Consequences of Modernity*. Basingstoke: Palgrave Macmillan.

Ferguson, H. and Kenny, P. (Eds.) (1995) *On Behalf of the Child: Child Welfare, Child Protection and the Child Care Act 1991*. Dublin: Farmer.

Ferguson, H. and O'Reilly, M. (2001) *Keeping Children Safe: Child Abuse, Child Protection and the Promotion of Welfare*. Dublin: Farmar.

Figley, C.R. (1995) *Compassion Fatigue: Coping with Secondary Traumatic Stress Disorder in Those Who Treat the Traumatised*. New York: Bruner/Mazel.

Fox Harding, L. (1997) *Perspectives in Child Care Policy*. London: Longman.

Fraser, D. (1984) *The Evolution of the British Welfare State*. 2nd edn. London: Macmillan.

Freeman, I. (1996) Social Work Intervention in Child Abuse: An Ever Widening Net? *Child Abuse Review*, 5: 181–90.

Frost, N. and Harris, J. (1996) *Managing Residential Child Care*. Brighton: Pavilion.

Gans, H.J. (1972) The Positive Functions of Poverty. *American Journal of Sociology*, 78: 2.

Gibbons, J., Conroy, S. and Bell, C. (1995) *Operating the Child Protection System*. London: HMSO.

Giddens, A. (1984) *The Constitution of Society: Outline of the Theory of Structuration*. Cambridge: Policy Press.

Gill, O. and Jack, G. (2007) *The Child and the Family in Context: Developing Ecological Practice in Disadvantaged Communities*. Lyme Regis: Russell House Publishing.

Gilligan, R. (1995) Family Support and Child Welfare: Realising the Promise of the Child Care Act. In Ferguson, H. and Kenny, P. (Eds.) *On Behalf of the Child: Child Welfare, Child Protection and the Child Care Act 1991*. Dublin: Farmer.

Gilligan, R. (1998) The Importance of Schools and Teachers in Child Welfare. *Child and Family Social Work*, 3: 1, 13–25.

Gilligan, R. (1999) Working with Social Networks: Key Resources in Helping Children at Risk. In Hill, M. (Ed.) *Effective Ways of Working with Children and their Families*. London: Jessica Kingsley.

Gilligan, R. (2000) Adversity, Resilience and Young People: The Protective Value of Positive School and Spare Time Experiences. *Children and Society*, 14: 37–47.

Gilligan, R. (2000) Family Support: Issues and Protects. In Canavan, J., Dolan, P. and Pinkerton, J. (Eds) *Family Support: Direction from Diversity*. London: Jessica Kingsley.

Gilligan, R. (2001) *Promoting Resilience: A Resource Guide on Working with Children in the Care System*. London: BAAF.

Giovannoni, J. (1998) Definitional Issues in Child Maltreatment. In Cicchetti, D. and Carlson, V. *Child Maltreatment: Theory and Research on the Causes and Consequences of Child Abuse and Neglect*. Cambridge: Cambridge University Press.

Giovannoni, J. and Becerra, R. (1979) *Defining Child Abuse*. New York: Free Press.

Glass, N. (2001) What Works for Children: The Political Issues. *Children and Society*, 15: 14–20.

Gordon, D. and Gibbons. J. (1998) Placing Children on Child Protection Registers: Risk Indicators and Local Authority Differences. *British Journal of Social Work*, 28: 423–26.

Gordon, P. (2007) *Evidence-based Practice in Child Protection: The Queensland Context*. Paper presented at the Symposium on evidence-based practice. Families, Youth and Community Care, Queensland.

Government of Ireland (1991) *Child Care Act 1991*. Dublin: Stationary Office.

Greene, S., Kelly, R., Nixon, E., Borska, Z., Murphy, S., Daly, A., Whyte, J. and Murphy, C. (2007) *A Study of Intercountry Adoption Outcomes in Ireland*. Dublin: Children's Research Centre, Trinity College.

Greenfields, M. and Statham, J. (2004) *The Use of Child Protection Registers*. London: Thomas Coram Research Institute.

Gregg, P., Harkness, S. and Machin, S. (1999) *Child Development and Family Income*. York: Joseph Rowntree Foundation.

Hallett, C. (1995) *Inter-agency Co-operation in Child Protection*. London: HMSO.

Hardiker, P., Exton, K. and Barker, M. (1991) *Policies and Practices in Preventive Child Care*. Aldershot: Avebury.

Harlow, E. and Lawler, J. (2000) *Management, Social Work and Change*. Aldershot: Ashgate.

Harrison, P. (2003) *A Statistical Analysis of Child Abuse Reports and Child in Care 2002–3*. Dublin: Northern Area Health Board.

Harrison, P. (2006) *Managing Social Care: A Guide for New Managers*. Lyme Regis: Russell House Publishing.

Harrison, P. (2007) American Humane's 2007 Conference on Differential Response in Child Welfare. *Children Acts Advisory Board Newsletter*, 3: 3.

Harrison, P. (2008) In the Shadow of a Giant: The Fate of Social Services in a Health Care System that is Changing (again . . .). *Health Matters: Journal of the Health Management Institute of Ireland*. Nov/Dec.

Harrison, R., Mann, G., Murphy, M., Taylor, A. and Thompson, N. (2003) *Partnership Made Painless: A Joined-up Guide to Working Together*. Lyme Regis: Russell House Publishing.

Health Information and Quality Authority, Social Services Inspectorate (2007) *The Placement of Children Aged 12 and Under in Residential Care in Ireland*. Dublin: HIQA, SSI.

Health Information and Quality Authority, Social Services Inspectorate (2007) *Inspection of the Health Service Executive Fostering Service in the Meath Local Health Area*. Dublin: HIQA, SSI.

Health Service Executive (2005) *Preliminary Analysis of Child Care Interim Dataset*. Dublin: HSE.

Health Service Executive (2005) *Review of Adequacy Report*. Dublin: HSE.

Health Service Executive (2006) *Review of Adequacy Report* Dublin: HSE.

Health Service Executive (2007) *Non-medical Male Circumcision: Report to Expert Advisory Group (Children)*. Dublin: HSE.

Health Service Executive (2007) *Transformation Programme 2007–2010*. Dublin: HSE.

Health Service Executive (2008) *Quarterly Child Care Performance Indicators*. Dublin: HSE.

Healy, L.M. and Pine, B.A. (2007) Ethical Issues for Social Work and Social Care Managers. In Aldgate, J. et al. (Eds.) *Enhancing Social Work Management*. London: Jessica Kingsley.

Hendrick, H. (1994) *Child Welfare England 1872–1989*. London: Routledge.

Hendrick, H. (1997) *Children, Childhood and English* Society. Cambridge: Cambridge University Press.

Hickman, G.R. and Lee, D.S. (2001) *Managing Human Resources in the Public Sector: A Shared Responsibility*. Fort Worth: Harcourt College Publishers.

Hill, M. (Ed.) (1995) *Effective Ways of Working with Children and Their Families*. London: Jessica Kingsley.

HM Government (2003) *Every Child Matters*. London: HMSO.

HM Government (2008) *National Indicators of Local Authorities and Local Authority Partnerships: Handbook of Definitions*. London: HMSO.

Horwath, J. (2002) Maintaining a Focus on the Child. *Abuse Review*, 11: 195–213.

Horwath, J. and Bishop, B. (2001) *Child Neglect: Is my View Your View? Working with Cases of Child Neglect in the North Eastern Health Board*. North Eastern Health Board/University of Sheffield.

Huxley, P. et al. (2005) Stress and Pressure in Mental Health Social Work: The Worker Speaks. *British Journal of Social Work*, 35: 1063–79.

International Federation of Social Work www.ifsw.org (Accessed May 1st, 2008)

International Society for the Prevention of Child Abuse and Neglect (2006) *World Perspectives on Child Abuse: An International Resource Book*. 7th edn. Chicago: ISPCAN.

Iwaniec, D. (1995) *The Emotionally Abused and Neglected Child: Identification, Assessment and Intervention*. Chichester: John Wiley.

Jack, G. (2006) The Area and Community Components of Children's Well-being. *Children and Society*, 20: 334–47.

Johnson, K. and Williams, I. (2007) *Managing Uncertainty and Change in Social Work and Social Care*. Lyme Regis: Russell House Publishing.

Johnson, S. and Petrie, S. (2004) Child Protection and Risk Management: The Death of Victoria Climbié. *Journal of Social Policy*, 33: 2, 179–202.

Johnson, S., Cooper, C., Cartwright, S., Donald, I., Taylor, P. and Millet, C. (2005) The Experience of Work-related Stress Across Occupations. *Journal of Managerial Psychology*, 20: 2, 178–87.

Jones, C. (2001) Voices from the Front Line: State Social Workers and New Labour. *British Journal of Social Work*, 31: 4, 547–62.

Jones, F., Fletcher, C. and Ibbetson, K. (1991) Stressors and Strains Among Social Workers: Demands, Supports, Constraints and Psychological Health. *British Journal of Social Work*.

Jones, J. and Gallop, L. (2003) No Time to Think: Protecting the Reflective Space in Children's Services. *Child Abuse Review*, 12: 101–6.

Jones, R. (2009) No Substitute for Experience. *The Guardian*, January 14th.

Kadushin, A. (1985) *Child Welfare Services*. 3rd edn. New York: Macmillan.

Kadushin, A. (1992) *Supervision in Social Work*. New York: Columbia University Press.

Kanter, R.M., Stein, B.A. and Jick, T.D. (1992) *The Challenge of Organisational Change: How Companies Experience it and How Leaders Guide it*. New York: Free Press.

Kearney, P. (2004) Front Line Managers: The Mediators of Standards and the Quality of Practice. In Statham, D. (Ed.) *Managing Front Line Practice in Social Care*. London: Jessica Kingsley.

Kelmer-Pringle, M. (1974) *The Needs of Children*. London: Hutchinson.

Kempe, C.H. (1962) The Battered Baby Syndrome. *Journal of the American Medical Association*, 181, 17.

Ketter, P.M., Moroney, R.M. and Martin, L.L. (1999) *Designing and Managing Programmes: An Effectiveness-based Approach*. Thousand Oaks, CA: Sage.

Lawler, J. (2000) *The Rise of Managerialism in Social Work*. In Harlow, E. and Lawler, J. (Eds.) *Management, Social Work and Change*. Aldershot: Ashgate.

Learner, E. and Rosen, G. (2004) Managing Duty Teams in Children's Services. In Statham, D. (Ed.) *Managing Front Line Practice in Social Care*. London: Jessica Kingsley.

Little, M. (1999) Prevention and Early Intervention with Children in Need: Definitions, Principles and Examples of Good Practice. *Children and Society.* 13: 304–16.

Little, M. and Gibbons, J. (1993) Predicting the Rate of Children on the Child Protection Register. *Research, Policy and Planning,.* 10: 15–18.

Little, M. and Mount, K. (1999) *Prevention and Early Intervention with Children in Need.* Aldershot: Ashgate.

Locke, E.A. (1976) The Nature and Cause of Job Satisfaction. In Dunette, M.D. (Ed) *Handbook of Industrial and Organisational Psychology.* Chicago: Rand McNally.

Lord Laming (2003) *The Victoria Climbié Inquiry:* Report of an Inquiry by Lord Laming. London: HMSO.

Lucy, C. (1943) The Beveridge Report and Eire. *Studies, 32.*

MacDonald, J. (2003) *Understanding Total Quality Management in a Week.* 3rd edn. London: Hodder and Stoughton.

MacNab, E. (2006) *Strengths Based Assessment in Child Protection: What Variables Should be Present?* A dissertation submitted to the National University of Ireland, Dublin in part fulfilment of a degree of Masters of Social Science.

Madden, R.G. (2007) Liability and Safety Issues in Human Service Management. In Aldgate, J. *et al.* (Eds.) *Enhancing Social Work Management.* London: Jessica Kingsley.

Maguire, K. and Truscott, F. (2006) *Active Governance: The Value Added by Community in Governance by Local Strategic Partnerships.* York: Joseph Rowntree Foundation.

Maguire, M.J. and Cinneide, Ó. (2005) A Good Beating Never Hurt Anyone: The Punishment and Abuse of Children in Twentieth Century Ireland. *Journal of Social History*, Spring 635–52.

Magura, S. and Silverman Moses, B. (2001) *Outcome Measures for Child Welfare Services: Theory and Applications.* Washington DC: Child Welfare League of America.

Martin, L.L. and Kettner, P.M. (1997) Performance Measurement: The New Accountability. *Administration in Social Work*, 21: 1 17–29.

Maslach, C. and Jackson, S. (1981) The Measurement and Experience of Burnout. *Journal of Occupational Behaviour*, 2: 99–113.

Maslow, A.H. (1968) *Towards a Psychology of Being.* 2nd edn. New York: Van Nostraad Reinhold.

Masson, J. (1997) Introducing Non-punitive Approaches into Child Protection. In Parton, N. (1998) *Child Protection: Tensions, Contradictions and Possibilities.* London: Routledge.

Mattison, M. (2000) Ethical Decision Making: The Person in the Process. *Social Work*, 45, 3.

McAulliffe, D. (2005) Putting Ethics on the Organisational Agenda: The Social Work Ethics Audit on Trial. *Australian Social Work*, 58: 357.

McGhee, J. and Francis, J. (2003) Protecting Children in Scotland: Examining the Impact of the Children (Scotland) Act 1995. *Child and Family Social Work*, 8: 133–42.

McGuinness, C. (1993) *Report of the Kilkenny Incest Investigation.* Dublin: Stationery Office.

McKeown, K. (2001) *Fathers and Families: Research and Reflection on Key Questions.* Department of Health and Children. Dublin: Government Publications.

McLean, J. and Andrew, T. (2000) Commitment, Satisfaction, Stress and Control among Social Service Managers and Social Workers in the UK. *Administration in Social Work*, 23: 3–4, 93–117.

McNeish, D. and Newman, T. (2001) Involving Children and Young People in Decision Making. In McNeish, D., Newman, T. and Roberts, H. (Eds.) *What Works for Children? Effective Services for Children and Families.* Buckingham: Open University Press.

McWhinney, I.R. (1998) Primary Care: The Core Values. In Pringle, M. (Ed.) *Primary Care: Core Values.* London: BMJ Books.

Michie, S. (2002) Causes and Management of Stress at Work. *Occupational and Environmental Medicine*, 59: 67–72.

Mill, J.S. (1869) *On Liberty.* London: Longman, Roberts and Green.

Millham, S. *et al.* (1986) (Dartington Social Research Unit) *Lost in Care: The Problems of Maintaining Links Between Children in Care and their Families.* Aldershot: Ashgate.

Ministry of Child and Youth Services (2005) *Child Welfare Transformation 2005: A Strategic Plan for a Flexible, Sustainable and Outcome Oriented Service Delivery Model*. London, ON: Child Welfare Secretariat.

Ministry of Child Protection and Youth Services (2007) *Child Protection Standards in Ontario*. Ontario: MCPYS.

Ministry of Social Development, Child, Youth and Family (2007) *Leading for Outcomes, 2007–2010* Christchurch: Child, Youth and Family www.cyf.govt.nz/Reports (Accessed March 19th, 2007)

Mondy, L. and Mondy, S. (2004) Engaging the Community in Child Protection Programmes: The Experience of NEWPIN in Australia. *Child Abuse Review*, 13: 433–40.

Morgan, R. (2005) *Children's Rights Report: What Inspectors Say About the Work of Services for Young People Living Away from Home*. London: CSCI.

Morgan, R. (2006) *About Social Workers: A Children's Views Report*. Newcastle: CSCI.

Morris, K. and Tunnard, J. (1996) (Eds.) *Family Group Conferences: Messages from the UK: Practices and Research*. London: Family Rights Group.

Morrison, T. (1999) *Staff Supervision in Social Care: An Action Learning Approach*. Brighton: Pavilion.

Morrison, T. *et al.* (1990) *Children and Parental Participation in Case Conferences*. London: NSPCC.

Moss, B. (2007) *Values*. Lyme Regis: Russell House Publishing.

Munro, E. (1996) Avoidable and Unavoidable Harm in Child Protection Work. *British Journal of Social Work*, 26: 6, 793–808.

Munro, E. (2004) The Impact of Audit on Social Work Practice. *British Journal of Social Work*, 34, 1075–95.

Munro, E. (2005) Improving Practice: Child Protection as a Systems Problem. *Children and Youth Services Review*, 27: 375–91.

Munro, E. (2005) What Tools do We Need to Improve Identification of Child Abuse? *Child Abuse Review*, 14: 374–88.

Munro, E. (2008) Baby P Case: Child Protection Experts' Responses. In Benjamin, A. *The Guardian*, November 11th.

National Association of Social Workers (USA) www.socialworkers.org/pubs/code/code/asp (Accessed May 1st, 2008)

National Board for Safeguarding Children (in press) *Safeguarding Children: Standards and Guidance for the Catholic Church*. Maynooth: NBSC. www.catholicbishops.ie/safeguarding-children

National Network for Social Work Managers www.socialworkmanager.org.org/Standards.htm (Accessed May 1st, 2008)

NCH Action for Children (1996) *Children Still in Need: Refocusing Child Protection in the Context of Children in Need*. London: NCH Action for Children.

Nelson, S. and Baldwin, N. (2004) The Craigmiller Project: Neighbourhood Mapping to Improve Children's Safety from Sexual Crime. *Child Abuse Review*, 13, 415–25.

Nixon, P. (2007) Seen but Not Heard? Children and Young People's Participation in Family Group Decision Making: Concepts and Practice Issues. *Protecting Children*, 22: 1, 20–36.

Northern Area Health Board (2002) *Matching Needs and Services: Cases Held by Public Health Nurses*. Report of the Development Exercise Between the Northern Area Health Board and Dartington Social Research Unit. Dublin: NAHB.

O'Brien, V. (2000) *Family Group Conference: Pilot Project Evaluation Report*. Bray: East Coast Area Health Board.

Office of Minister for Children (2007) *Agenda for Children's Services*. Dublin: Office of Minister for Children.

Office of the First Minister and Deputy First Minister (2006) *Our Children and Young People: Our Pledge*. Belfast: Office of the First Minister and Deputy First Minister. www.allchildrenni.gov.uk/tenyear-strategychildren1pdf (Accessed March 19th, 2007)

Ofsted, Healthcare Commission and HM Inspectorate of Constabulary (2008) *Joint Review: Haringey Children's Services Authority Area: Review of Services for Children and Young People, with Particular Reference to Safeguarding*. Manchester: Ofsted.

Oliver, C. *et al.* (2001) *Figures and Facts: Local Authority Variance on Indicators Concerning Child Protection and Children Looked After.* London: Tomas Coram Research Centre, University of London.

Onyango, P. and Lynch, M.A. (2006) Implementing the Right to Child Protection: A Challenge for Developing Countries. *The Lancet*, 367, February 25.

Ó'Riordáin, S. (2006) *Poverty and Social Inclusion: Linking Local and National Structures.* Dublin: Combat Poverty Agency.

Packman, J. (1981) *The Child's Generation: Child Care Policy in Britain.* Oxford: Blackwell.

Packman, J. and Hall, C. (1998) *From Care to Accommodation: Support, Protection and Control in Child Care Services.* London: HMSO.

Packman, J. with Randall, J. and Jacques, N. (1986) *Who Needs Care? Social Work Decisions About Children.* Oxford: Basil Blackwell.

Parker, R., Ward, H. Jackson, S., Aldgate, J. and Wedge, P. (Eds.) (1995) *Looking After Children: Assessing Outcomes in Child Care.* London: HMSO.

Parton, N. (1991) *Governing the Family: Child Care, Child Protection and the State.* London: Macmillan.

Parton, N. (1998) Risk, Advanced Liberalism and Child Welfare: The Need to Rediscover Uncertainty and Ambiguity. *British Journal of Social Work*, 28: 1, 5–27.

Parton, N. (2002) Protecting Children: A Socio-historical Analysis. In Wilson, K. and James, A. *The Child Protection Handbook*, 2nd edn. Edinburgh: Baillière Tindall.

Parton, N. (2004) From Maria Colwell to Victoria Climbié: Reflections on Public Inquiries into Child Abuse a Generation Apart. *Child Abuse Review*, 13: 80–94.

Parton, N. (Ed.) (1997) *Child Protection and Family Support: Tensions, Contradictions and Possibilities* London: Routledge.

Parton. N. and Mathews, R. (2001) New Directions in Child Protection and Family Support in Western Australia: A Policy Initiative to Re-focus Child Welfare Practice. *Child and Family Social Work*, 6, 97–113.

Percy-Smith, J. (2006) What Works in Strategic Partnerships for Children: A Research Review. *Children and Society*, 20: 313–23.

Peters, T.J. and Waterman, R.H. Jr., (1982) *In Search of Excellence*. New York: Harper and Row.

Pinkerton, J., Higgins, K. and Devine, P. (2000) *Family Support: Linking Project Evaluation to Policy Analysis.* Ashgate: Aldershot.

Platt, D. (2001) Refocusing Children's Services: Evaluation of an Initial Assessment Process. *Child and Family Social Work*, 6: 139–48.

Platt, D. (2006) Threshold Decisions: How Social Workers Prioritize Referrals of Child Concern. *Child Abuse Review*, 15: 4–18.

Pringle, M. (1986) 3rd edn. *The Needs of Children.* London: Routledge.

Pugh, R. (2007) Variations in Registration on Child Protection Registers. *British Journal of Social Work*, 37, 5–21.

Qiao, D.P. and Chan, Y.C. (2005) Child Abuse in China: A Yet-to-be-acknowledged 'Social Problem' in the Chinese Mainland. *Child and Family Social Work*, 10: 21–7.

Reamer, F.G. (1998) The Evolution of Social Work Ethics. *Social Work*, 43: 6.

Residential Institutions Redress Board (2008) www.rirb.ie Accessed March 17th 2008.

Roberts, H. and Roberts, I. (2000) Smacking. *Child: Care, Health and Development.* 26: 4, 259–62.

Rose, M. (2003) Good Deal, Bad Deal? Job Satisfaction in Occupations. *Work, Employment and Society.* 17: 3, 503–30.

Rose, W., Aldgate, J. and Barns, J. (2007) *From Policy Visions to Practice Realities: The Pivotal Role of Service Managers in Implementation.* In Aldgate, J. et al. *Enhancing Social Work Management: Theory and Best Practice from the UK and USA.* London: Jessica Kingsley.

Rosenbeg, G. and Holden, G. (1992) Social Work Effectiveness: A Response to Cheetham. *Research on Social Work Practice*, 2: 3, 288–96.

Rosenberg, F., Bellonci, C., Cooney, M. and Bray, J. (2007) *Stories from Residential Treatment: New Pathways to Family Support.* Child Welfare League of America.

Rowntree, B.S. (1901) *Poverty: A Study of Town Life.* London: Macmillan.

Safeguarding Children (2005) *Second Joint Chief Inspector's Report on Safeguarding Children*. Commission for Social Inspection.

Sanders, R., Jackson, S. and Thomas, N. (1997) Policy Priorities in Child Protection: Perception of Risk and Agency Strategy. *Policy Studies*, 18: 2, 139–58.

Sarri, R. and Hasenfeld, Y. (Eds.) (1978) *The Management of Human Services*. New York: Columbia Press.

Scott, J., Moore, T. and Ward, H. (2005) Evaluating Interventions and Monitoring Outcomes. In Scott, J. and Ward, H. *Safeguarding and Promoting the Well-being of Children, Families and Communities*. London: Jessica Kingsley.

Scragg, T. (2005) *Managing at the Front Line: A Handbook for Managers in Social Care Agencies*. Brighton: Pavilion.

Sinclair, R. and Franklin, A. (2001) *Children's Participation. What Works? Messages From Research*. London: National Children's Bureau.

Smith, R. (2005). *Values and Practice in Children's Services*. Basingstoke: Palgrave Macmillan.

Smith, T. (1999) Neighbourhood and Preventative Strategies with Children and Families: What Works? *Children and Society*, 13: 265–77.

Social Service Inspectorate (2003) *Report on the Monitoring of the Implementation of Children First: National Guidelines for the Protection and Welfare of Children*. Dublin: SSI.

Social Service Inspectorate (2004) *Building a Better Future for Children: Key Messages from Inspection and Performance Assessment*. London: DoH.

Social Service Inspectorate (2006) *Our Children and Young People: Our Shared Responsibility*. Northern Ireland: DoH, Social Services and Public Safety.

Spratt, T. and Callan, J. (2004) Parents' Views on Social Work Interventions in Child Welfare Cases. *British Journal of Social Work*, 34, 199–224.

Spratt, T. (2000) Decision Making by Senior Social Workers at the Point of First Referral. *British Journal of Social Work*, 30: 597–618.

Spratt, T. (2001) The Influence of Child Protection Orientation on Child Welfare Practice. *British Journal of Social Work*, 31: 933–54.

Stanley, J. and Goddard, C. (2002) *In the Firing Line: Violence and Power in Child Protection Work*. Chichester: Wiley.

Stanley, N., Manthorpe, J. and White, M. (2006) Depression in the Profession: Social Workers' Experiences and Perceptions. *British Journal of Social Work*, 37: 281–98.

Statham, D. (Ed.) (2004) *Managing Front Line Practice in Social Care*. London: Jessica Kingsley.

Statham, J., Candappa, M. and Owen, C. (2002) *Trends in Care: Exploring Reasons for the Increase in Children Looked After by Local Authorities*. London: Tomas Coram Research Centre, University of London Institute of Education.

Staub, E. (2003) *The Psychology of Good and Evil: Why Children, Adults and Groups Help and Harm Others*. Cambridge: Cambridge University Press.

Sullivan, H. and Skelcher, C. (2002) *Working Across Boundaries: Collaboration in Public Services*. London: Palgrave Macmillan.

Sylva, K. (1994) School Influence on Child Development. *Journal of Child Psychology and Psychiatry*, 35: 135–72.

Tanner, K. and Turney, D. (2003) What do we Know About Child Neglect? A Critical Review of the Literature and its Application to Social Work Practice. *Child and Family Social Work*, 8, 25–34.

Taylor, S. (2002) *The Employee Retention Handbook*. London: Chartered Institute of Personnel and Development.

Tennyson, R. (1998) *Managing Partnerships: Tools for Mobilising the Public Sector, Business and Civil Society as Partners in Development*. Prince of Wales Business Leaders Forum.

Testra, M. and Furstenberg, F. (2002) The Social Ecology of Child Endangerment. In Roseenheim, F. *et al.* (Eds) *A Century of Juvenile Justice*. Chicago: University of Chicago Press.

Tham, P. (2007) Why Are They Leaving? Factors Affecting Intention to Leave Among Social Workers in Child Welfare. *British Journal of Social Work*, 37, 1225–46.

The Second Joint Chief Inspector's Report (2005) *Safeguarding Children*. London: DoH.

Thoburn, J., Lewis, A. and Shemmings, D. (1995) *Paternalism or Partnership? Family Involvement in the Child Protection Process. Studies in Child Protection*. London: HMSO.

Thompson, N. (2005) *Understanding Social Work: Preparing for Practice*. 2nd edn. London: Palgrave.

Thompson, N., Murphy, M. and Stradling, S. (1994) *Dealing with Stress*. Basingstoke: Macmillan.

Tilbury, C. (2004) The Influence of Performance Measurement on Child Welfare Policy and Practice. *British Journal of Social Work*, 34: 225–41.

Tilbury, C. (2007) The Regulation of Out of Home Care. *British Journal of Social Work*, 37: 209–24.

Toubia, N. (1994) Female Circumcision as a Public Health Issue. *The New England Journal of Medicine*, 313: 11, 712–16.

Trocmé , N., Knott, D. and Knoke, D. (2003) *An Overview of Differential Response Models*, Toronto, ON: Centre of Excellence for Child Welfare, University of Toronto, www.cecw-cepb.ca

Tunstill, J. (1997) *Implementing the Family Support Clauses of the 1989 Children Act.*

Tunstill, J. and Aldgate, J. (2000) *Services for Children in Need: From Policy to Practice*. London: HMSO.

Turner, K. and Turney, D. (2003) What do we Know about Child Neglect? A Critical Review of the Literature and its Application to Social Work Practice. *Child and Family Social Work*, 8: 25–34.

UNICEF (1989) *UN International Convention on the Rights of the Child*. New York:UNICEF.

UNICEF (2005) *Child Poverty in Rich Countries*. London: UNICEF.

UNICEF (2008) *The State of the World's Children: Child Survival*. London: UNICEF.

US Advisory Board on Child Abuse and Neglect (1993) *Neighbors Helping Neighbors: Foundations for a New National Strategy*. Washington: US Government Printing Office.

Utting, W. (1991) *Children in the Public Care: A Review of Residential Child Care*. London: HMSO.

Utting, W. (1997) *People Like Us. The Report of the Review Safeguards of Children Living Away from Home*. London: HMSO.

Walker, S. and Thurston, C. (2006) *Safeguarding Children and Young People: A Guide to Integrated Practice*. Lyme Regis: Russell House Publishing.

Ward, H. (2004) Working with Managers to Improve Services: Changes in the Role of Research in Social Care. *Child and Family Social Work*, 9: 99, 13–25.

Wattam, C. (1999) The Prevention of Child Abuse. *Children and Society*, 13: 317–29.

Webb, S.A. (2001) Some Considerations on the Validity of Evidence-based Practice in Social Work. *British Journal of Social Work*, 31: 57–9.

Westbrook, T.M., Ellis, J. and Ellett, A.J. (2006) Improving Retention Among Public Child Welfare Workers: What Can we Learn from Insights and Experiences of Committed Survivors. *Administration in Social Work*, 30: 4.

Whyte, J.H. *Church and State in Modern Ireland 1923–1979*. 2nd edn. Dublin: Gill and Macmillan.

Williams, M.C. (1997) *Parents, Children and Social Workers – Working in Partnership under the Children Act 1989*. Aldershot: Avebury.

Willumsen, E. and Skivenes, M. (2005) Collaboration Between Service Users and Professionals: Legitimate Decisions in Child Protection: A Norwegian Model. *Child and Family Social Work*, 10: 197–206.

Winter, K. (2006) Widening our Knowledge Concerning Young Looked After Children: The Case for Research using Sociological Models of Childhood. *Child and Family Social Work*, 11: 55–64.

Winter, K. and Connolly, P. (2005) A Small Scale Study of the Relevance Between Measures of Deprivation and Child-Care Referrals. *British Journal of Social Work*, 35, 937–53.

Wolmar, C. (2000) *Forgotten Children: The Secret Abuse Scandal in Children's Homes*. London: Vision Paperbacks.

Woodroofe, K. (1962) *From Charity to Social Work in England and the United States*. London: Routledge and Kegan Paul.

World Health Organisation (1999) *Report of the Consultation on Child Abuse Prevention*. Geneva: WHO.

World Health Organisation (2002) *World Report on Violence and Health*. Geneva: WHO.

Wright, S. (2004) Child Protection in the Community: A Community Development Approach. *Child Abuse Review*, 13: 384–98.

Yoshikawa, H. (1994) Prevention as Cumulative Protection: Effects of Early Family Support and Education on Chronic Delinquency and its Risks. *Psychological Bulletin*, 115: 28–54.

Young, A.F. and Ashton, E.T. (1956) *British Social Work in the 19th Century*. London: Routledge and Kegan Paul.